the
CHRISTIAN
at
Play

Robert K. Johnston

WILLIAM B. EERDMANS PUBLISHING COMPANY
GRAND RAPIDS, MICHIGAN

To Margaret
May she always play (and work)
with childlike abandon

The Scripture quotations in this book
are from the Revised Standard Version of the Bible,
copyrighted 1946, 1952, © 1971, 1973.

Library of Congress Cataloging in Publication Data
Johnston, Robert K., 1945-
The Christian at play.

Bibliography: p. 163
1. Play—Religious aspects—Christianity. 2. Work
(Theology) I. Title.
BT709.J63 1983   233   83-16552
ISBN 0-8028-1976-1

Contents

Preface

IT WAS THE LATE PAUL TILLICH WHO, MORE THAN ANY
other modern theologian, introduced Christians to the need for
a theology of culture. Writing from a liberal Protestant perspective, he attempted to show the religious dimensions of our varied
cultural activity, to illuminate the spiritual lines that oftentimes
lie hidden within our human creations. Evangelical Christians
have been slow to follow Tillich's lead. Perhaps fearing another
"social gospel," evangelicals have focused too exclusively upon
humankind's sinfulness, overlooking its God-given creativity. The
result has been a skewing of the Christian understanding of
"man."

Play, as an event of the inventive human spirit, invites our
most able Christian reflection. The person at play is expressing
his or her God-given nature. Yet as Christians we have largely
overlooked this aspect of our creaturehood. We will need to
define "play" with much greater care as we proceed, but it is
useful at the outset to note several of its chief dimensions. First,
play is a comprehensive human experience. Involving not only
the body but the emotions and the mind, play affords at least a
momentary integration of life.

Play has a social aspect as well, its delight finding its center
not in the player but in that *with* which he plays. Whether this
be a co-player, a baseball, or a phonograph record, the value of
play is located first of all in the other. Moreover, students of
play have recognized that play's personal and social dimensions
have consequences beyond themselves. The "other" which is
experienced by the fully involved player is not merely the co-player
or play object. Play oftentimes pushes the individual outward
beyond his or her normally perceived world, enlarging that
understanding of reality in the process. It is this "result" of play
which some have found to have particular theological relevance
and which this book will explore.

Prior to such investigation, however—prior to a discussion
of play's basis in and witness to common grace—we need to

allow play to be viewed as the "end in itself" which it is. Play is an activity with its own purposes and inner rewards. It needs no justification beyond itself. To move too quickly to play's consequences is to risk aborting the play activity, turning it into a disguised instance of work. The Christian is called to work; but he is also meant to play.

The Academy Award-winning film *Chariots of Fire* (1982) illustrates well the value of play for its own sake. The movie tells the story of two runners who competed in the 1924 Olympics, Harold Abrahams and Eric Liddell. Abrahams, a Jew among Gentiles, runs for his country *in order to* prove his worth to his English countrymen. Only by being a success can he overcome the anti-Semitism directed at him. When his girlfriend asks him if he loves to run, he responds, "I'm more an addict. It's a compulsion. A weapon." As he waits for the finals of the one-hundred-yard dash, he tells his friend that he is scared: "Ten lonely seconds to justify my existence." And Abrahams does just that. He wins the gold medal. Having proven his worth through running, Harold Abrahams can give it up, and he does. His job has been completed.

Eric Liddell, on the other hand, runs for the sheer pleasure of it, so much so that his austere, religious sister criticizes him. "I don't want his work spoiled with all this running talk," she says. In a poignant moment in the film, Liddell tells his sister that he has decided to return to China to serve as a missionary. She is overjoyed until he adds, "I've got a lot of running to do first. Jenny, Jenny, you've got to understand it. I believe that God made me for a purpose—for China. But he also made me fast. And when I run I feel his pleasure . . . it's not just fun. To win is to honor him." Liddell does win—the four-hundred-meter dash—and it does bring honor to his Lord. As the film ends, we are told that after the Olympics Liddell returned to China as he said he would. His season of play over, he is able to find a similar joy in his work, knowing that it, too, is a part of life's God-intended rhythm. Eric Liddell understood what many Christians do not: that we are called not only to work but to play.

This book is the product of several influences. Like Michael Novak, I too wonder how I can be almost forty and still care what happens to the Dodgers. How is the Christian to understand his love for handball? Or opera? Or stamp collecting? Or reading? It was Robert McAfee Brown, an instructor at Stanford University, who first provided some clues for me in a course entitled "Theology and Contemporary Literature." Could God use modern writers of fiction, or perhaps even baseball players, much as he used the Assyrians in Isaiah's day, to communicate his truth to us? My investigation of play continued at Duke University, where I wrote my dissertation, *Theology and Play,* under Thomas Langford. There I learned that we need to let our play remain just what it is—play. (Evangelical Christians in particular are so prone to instrumentalize everything.)

My investigation of the Christian at play might have stopped at this stage except for two factors: (1) there is little or no serious theological reflection currently focusing on our play (or our work!), and (2) Americans in particular continue to find it difficult to give themselves freely and/or authentically to their play. I am convinced that these two factors are related. Unable to understand our play as God-given, we remain inauthentic players. Thus, after a hiatus of eight years, I have returned to the topic of the Christian at play in the hopes of contributing to the well-being of Christ's Church. We are, as Christians, created to work *and* to play.

I have had several graduate students help with this project: Bob O'Connor, Webb Mealy, Scott Colglazier, and Bill Watkins. In addition, Arvin Vos and Robert Roberts have read the manuscript and offered helpful suggestions. In February 1982, Southwestern Baptist Theological Seminary kindly invited me to give the Day-Higginbotham Lectures on the topic of this book. I benefited greatly from my interaction with students and faculty at that institution, which is in the forefront of education in church recreation. Finally, I would like to thank my typists: Robin Wright, Lorie Poole, and Anne Stevenson.

ROBERT K. JOHNSTON
North Park Theological Seminary
Chicago, Illinois
December 1982

I wonder whether it is possible (it almost seems so today) to regain the idea of the Church as providing an understanding of the area of freedom (art, education, friendship, play), so that Kierkegaard's "aesthetic existence" would not be banished from the Church's sphere, but would be reestablished within it? I really think that is so, and it would mean that we should recover a link with the Middle Ages. Who is there, for instance, in our times, who can devote himself with an easy mind to music, friendship, games, or happiness? Surely not the "ethical" man, but only the Christian.

—**Dietrich Bonhoeffer,**
January 23, 1944, *Letters and Papers from Prison*

How could I be forty years old and still care what happens to the Dodgers?

—**Michael Novak**
The Joy of Sports

Introduction

IN ADDRESSING THE TOPIC OF THE CHRISTIAN AT PLAY, one risks inadvertently writing another "Pop Theology." American theology of recent vintage can perhaps best be described as "movement" theology. In the last twenty years, we have had theologies of the death of God, of secularity, of revolution, of culture, of hope, of process, of story, of human potential, and so on. One of the most interesting of these theological fads has centered on the human as player. Each avant-garde trend has raised important issues, but all have proven ephemeral, including theologies of play. Too often they have mistakenly baptized current opinion and made it identical with the Christian faith.[1]

Commenting on this trend in American popular theology, Thomas Oden concludes:

> Bandwagon "wave-of-the-future" theology has proven to be a very hazardous occupation in an era of accelerating change, especially when the continuities of history are not as evident as its discontinuities, and when the media focus the public eye upon society's distortions rather than its solidities.[2]

Oden goes on to ask, "What is the appropriate response to such developments?" And he answers, "The same as before. The task of theology still remains to make self-consistent and intelligible the life of faith in Christian community."[3] Theology today must attempt to reappropriate Christian tradition and biblical faith in terms of our contemporary situation and language. Theology can be faithful to itself only as it fully takes into account both Scripture and tradition as well as humankind's present predicament and possibility.

Like Oden, I do not share the belief of some of my contemporaries that constructive Christian thinking—that is, theology—is no longer possible, and that play is all that is humanly supportable.[4] Nor do I care to become "deliciously irresponsible" and merely produce fantasies about fun and frolics on the beach or in the bedroom, of leisure filled with ecstasy and laughter.[5] Rather, my concern in this book is to inquire on behalf of the Christian community about the significance of play. What is there that is theologically important about the person (both Christian and non-Christian) at play?

From the time of Augustine down to the present era, Christians have often been suspicious of play. For Augustine, conversion to Christianity meant a conversion *from* a life of play. To him, even eating was sinful if done in a spirit of pleasure.[6] The only enjoyment Augustine allowed for was the enjoyment of God. In varying degrees, such an assessment of play has plagued Christianity down to the present. It is often thought that in play one risks being uninvolved and irresponsible. The evils of play's misuse have been judged more severely than the perversions of work. It is safer to spend one's time in "serious" activity than to enter into "frivolity."

However, Christians today are rediscovering the need to play. In a world in which our work gravitates toward the extremes of ulcers or boredom, play becomes the possibility for discovering our common humanity. In a world that has become objectivized and routinized, play offers freedom to the human spirit. In a time when the richness of play (from recreational activity to the arts) is available to an increasing number of Americans, and when some are finding sources of pleasure, meaning, and power within such experiences, Christian theology is being challenged to reassess its suspicions of play. Is there an alternative both to the traditional work ethic that has dominated Christian thought and to the hedonism and narcissism that characterizes much contemporary discussion of play? A theology of play need not be the latest outbreak of the fad syndrome. Instead, it might better be understood as the Christian community's serious attempt to develop a fuller understanding of one of life's possibilities: the person at play.

A brief description of my methodology is appropriate as we begin. How do I understand the theological task, particularly as it relates to the phenomenon of play? Theology always originates from a given *tradition*; it also emerges within a particular historical *context*. As such, it is never merely the repetition of *biblical ideas* alone, even for those holding to the sole and binding authority of Scripture as God's revelation. *The work of theology consists of an ongoing dialogue between biblical, traditional, and contemporary sources.* For the evangelical theologian, this dialogue will ultimately be submitted to the final authority of Scripture, but a spirited interaction between all three of theology's sources can never be cut short.

As I have argued in a previous book, *Evangelicals at an Impasse: Biblical Authority in Practice,* there is no set procedure or program for controlling this theological dialogue. One does not always begin from the biblical text, for example; "theology remains an 'art' in that the proper valuation and interaction of its sources demand a wisdom that defies a comprehensive codification."[7] Sometimes new biblical data will provide the occasion for theological reflection. Such has been the case in recent discussions about the role of women in the church and the family. Sometimes a confrontation between competing Christian traditions will raise the challenge for theological reassessment. The Christian's rightful role vis-à-vis the state would seem one recent subject for Christian reflection where differences in traditional formulations have proven decisive. And who can dispute the fact that pressure from our wider culture has been the major catalyst behind continuing Christian discussion about the Church and the homosexual?

The key to creative Christian thinking is the willingness to live with theology's multiple sources while accepting Scripture's ultimate authority. Such an "evangelical" agenda rejects conservative methodologies that are content to recycle past truths without processing them afresh through contemporary sensibilities, alternative Christian traditions, and developing biblical understandings. It also rejects liberal methodologies that remain satisfied with adjudicating between competing theological sources according to the latest popular notion about what is reasonable. Christian theology must remain humble enough for its multiple sources to correct previous but faulty judgments. It must also remain faithful enough to trust Scripture to have the final word.

In approaching a theology of play in this book, we will begin with the problem which play poses to the contemporary person. For although our work-dominated values concerning the nature of humankind seem to be in transition, Americans remain curiously ill-prepared to play authentically. Either we work at work or we work at play—this in spite of the fact that leisure is ours in ever-increasing measure. As a result, we compromise the place of play in our lives.

After exploring current attitudes toward and descriptions of play, we will turn to three representative theological positions in hope of clarifying our understanding of the human player. Is play to be the Christian's life-style, as Sam Keen argues; the Christian's mission, as Jurgen Moltmann suggests; or the Christian's opportunity, as C. S. Lewis describes it?

Dialogue between these competing theological options challenges one to take a fresh look at the biblical record in the hope of uncovering new insights concerning the shape God intended human life to take. Thus we will turn next to a reassessment of the Bible's notion of play. Although play is an incidental concern of those writers focusing upon redemption and covenant, it is central to the creation theology of the Old Testament (e.g., in Ecclesiastes and the Song of Songs), as well as to discussions of the Sabbath. Moreover, in considering such biblical topics as festival, dance, feasting, hospitality, and friendship, new perspectives on play do indeed surface. Within the biblical text can be found a God-intended shape for human life which maintains a crucial balance between work and play. We are not merely workers, as some have insisted. We are also players who find life (including our work) both relativized and refreshed by play.

In the final chapter of this book, the discussion of the person at play will again be related to the world of work, this time within a biblical framework. In this way the beginning of a hermeneutical circle will be suggested. As René Padilla has argued,

> . . . the contextual approach to the interpretation of Scripture involves a dialogue between the historical situation and Scripture, a dialogue in which the interpreters approach Scripture with a particular perspective (their world-and-life view) and approach their situation with a particular comprehension of the Word of God (their theology). . . .[8]

Theological hermeneutics should have a "spiral structure" in which there is ongoing circulation between culture, tradition, and biblical text, each enriching the understanding of the other. Thus contemporary attitudes and practices of play will not only direct our inquiry into theological and biblical sources; they will themselves be challenged and redirected by the insights gained by the Christian community in dialogue with Scripture.

I

Play:
A Problem for the
Contemporary Person

The Leisure Revolution: Fact or Myth?

IT HAS BECOME ALMOST A TRUISM TO SPEAK OF present-day American culture as leisure-oriented. While leisure itself is not new, modern social critics have widely observed that leisure in America has taken on a uniqueness and increased relevance because it is no longer a luxury allowed only to the social elite. In medieval times, tournaments were limited to the nobility. In 1541, Henry VIII restricted bowling to aristocrats and property-owners (not beer-drinkers!). In Virginia in 1674, a tailor was fined for racing his horse against a gentleman's. But things have changed. Having become a part of the lives of the masses, leisure presents Americans with a situation that is historically new.

There are many indicators of the increase of leisure time in America. For example, Joseph Zeisel has studied American industry during the period from 1850 to 1956, and has documented the continuing long-term decline in the industrial workweek.[1] Whereas in 1850 the average worker put in sixty-six hours a week (i.e., eleven hours a day, six days a week), in 1956 the average worker in non-agricultural industries generally worked about forty hours (i.e., eight hours a day, five days a week).

Staffan Linder questions the conclusions often drawn from such statistics, however. If we look at the figures since 1929, he says, the average workweek has changed little. Furthermore, "the spreading practice of part-time work among women and teen-agers is causing a reduction in the average workweek as statistically measured, without this reality signifying any decline in work input. . . ."[2] Linder's rejoinder has proven itself valid, as more recent studies confirm the stabilization of the workweek at about forty hours. Nevertheless, for most Americans the introduction and continued development of vacations with pay, paid holidays, and sick leave have meant an increasing number of hours spent outside the workplace. In 1956 the average worker had twenty such days a year.[3] Marion Clawson, a contributor to the study *Leisure in America: Blessing or Curse?,* has projected that by the year 2000, paid time off the job will be almost five times what it was in 1950.[4] This prediction is already a reality for some factory workers with high seniority, who receive up to thirteen weeks off with pay.

Perhaps even more significant than the increase in fringe benefits is the changing timespan of people's working lives and the ratio of working to non-working years during the life cycle. Whereas the typical worker at the turn of the century began his life task early in his youth and died while employed or soon after retiring, the worker of today begins his or her vocation later in the life cycle, after an extended period of education, and retires earlier, with the prospect of many active years still ahead. Thus, according to a Congressional report made in 1973 entitled *Work in America,* "in 1900, two-thirds of American men who were 65 years of age and older were working. By 1971, the figure had dropped to one-fourth, with a smaller proportion on a year-round, fulltime basis."[5] These statistics take on even more significance when combined with the following two. Whereas in 1900 America had only 3 million people over sixty-five years of age, in 1980 the figure had risen to 25.5 million people, nine percent of the entire population. Moreover, whereas in 1900 the average life expectancy was 47.3 years, in 1978 it had risen dramatically to 73.3 years.

As time off from the job increases, so, it seems, does participation in various forms of recreation. In fact, leisure-time activities have become the nation's leading industry as measured by people's spending. Whereas in 1965 roughly 58 billion dollars was spent on leisure pursuits, that figure had grown to an estimated 244 billion dollars in 1981, 77 billion more than was spent on national defense. This was an increase of 321 percent in just sixteen years, an increase that far outdistanced inflation's gains. Leisure accounts for one of every eight dollars spent by the American consumer, and even increased inflation and tightening monetary conditions have changed the pattern little. When people cut back, vacations are usually the last budget item to go. During the recessionary period of 1979, for example, sales of sporting goods increased from $8 billion to $8.6 billion. Attendance at sporting events rose 45 percent—to 314 million people—between 1966 and 1976. Forty percent of all Americans are involved in some craft; fifty percent are amateur gardeners. Participatory sports are booming: swimming (105 million), bicycling (70 million), and camping (60 million) lead the way, but jogging is up from insignificant participation in 1973 to over 36 million runners today; 28 million more play softball. More passive leisure activities are increasingly popular, too: American sales of home electronic equipment totaled 25 billion dollars in 1981. Americans are spending more time and money on non-work activities than any other people. And the boom shows no sign of slackening.

New opportunities for recreation, as well as for travel, education, and entertainment, have become available chiefly because of the continued increase in the average American's purchasing power. From 1950 to 1979 the actual purchasing power of the average American family rose by 97 percent. Using a constant dollar pegged to the 1979 inflation level, one notes a steady rise in consumer purchasing power as the median family income increased from $10,008 in 1950, to $13,774 in 1960, to $18,444 in 1970, and to $19,684 in 1979. It is true that the average annual percentage increase in family income since 1970 (0.8%) has not kept pace with the growth of that income in the 60's (3.0% yearly). Nevertheless, Americans have more to spend than ever before, a fact that has encouraged a wide range of leisure pursuits.

Observers of work and leisure in American life often note that in conjunction with the increase in purchasing power, paid holidays, leisure time, and recreational activity, and with the shorter workweek, there has also been for many an unfortunate decrease in the meaningfulness of work itself. Many people are turning to leisure activity in an attempt to overcome the anonymity and routine associated with their jobs. Millions perceive work as too supervised, too compartmentalized, or too insecure. For them it is just a job that involves marking time. The Congressional study *Work in America* concluded:

> And significant numbers of American workers are dissatisfied
> with the quality of their working lives. Dull, repetitive, seemingly
> meaningless tasks, offering little challenge or autonomy, are caus-
> ing discontent among workers at all occupational levels. . . .
> . . . .
> Many workers at all occupational levels feel locked-in, their mo-
> bility blocked, the opportunity to grow lacking in their jobs, chal-
> lenge missing from their tasks.[6]

Apparently many people view work as merely a means to an
end. It is a way of acquiring purchasing power, but it is not, as
it was for many in previous generations, the center of one's
intimate human relationships nor the primary source of one's
feelings of enjoyment, happiness, and worth. When one reads
Studs Terkel's book, *Working,* a series of interviews with more
than 100 workers published in 1974, one gets the impression
that most people keep working for lack of alternatives, not because they get much fulfillment from their jobs. As Terkel himself writes,

> For many, there is a discontent. The blue-collar blues is no
> more bitterly sung than the white-collar moan. "I'm a machine,"
> says the spot-welder. "I'm caged," says the bank teller, and echoes
> the hotel clerk. "I'm a mule," says the steelworker. "A monkey
> can do what I do," says the receptionist. "I'm less than a farm
> implement," says the migrant worker. "I'm an object," says the
> high-fashion model.[7]

As one worker explained it to Terkel, " 'Most of us . . . have jobs
that are too small for our spirit. Jobs are not big enough for
people.' "[8]

"The auto industry is the *locus classicus* of dissatisfying
work," according to the Congressional study cited above; "the
assembly-line, its quintessential embodiment. But what is strik-
ing is the extent to which the dissatisfaction of the assembly-line
and blue-collar worker is mirrored in white-collar and even man-
agerial positions."[9] Rather than developing the person, modern-
day employment has often turned the worker into a mere func-
tionary. In 1971 Joseph Dumazedier studied the industrial worker
in American society. His conclusion: "The majority of workers
and employees (blue collar and white collar) in American society
do not sense fulfillment of their personality in their work (sixty-
two percent of the blue collars and sixty-one percent of white
collars)."[10] His findings are in line with those of Richard Pfeffer,

whose book, *Working for Capitali$m*, paints a bleak picture indeed. Pfeffer writes:

> If work in America is as destructive as it is portrayed in this book, and if the quality of work in any society is indicative of the true nature of that society, then life in America in some substantive sense must be destructive, like work in America. . . . The undeniable and generally accepted truth concerning work in the United States today, is that, on the whole, it is extremely confining, dehumanized, and meaningless for those who perform it.[11]

How Leisurely Is Our Leisure Time?

> *In truth, for millions of Americans —*hard-working *Americans —leisure has come to mean little more than an ever more furious orgy of consumption. Whatever energies are left after working are spent in pursuing pleasure with the help of an endless array of goods and services. This is "virtuous materialism" par excellence. It offers men the choice of either working themselves to death or consuming themselves to death —or both.*
> —GORDON DAHL[12]

One can catalogue fairly easily, as I have done, such things as the shorter workweek, the earlier retirement age, the increase in vacation time and paid holidays, the greater consumer buying power, and the lack of fulfillment in work. These factors make seemingly impressive evidence that American society is moving from a work orientation toward a leisure orientation. But before any conclusions are drawn, several qualifications should be noted, because complications arise in the otherwise straightforward trend toward increased "play" in America. Any negative evidence has often been ignored by advocates of leisure, who have reported only half the story. We heard for years that the rubber workers in Akron, Ohio, with their traditional six-hour day, were in the vanguard of a more general movement toward reduced working hours. What was often not mentioned was that almost sixty percent of these six-hour-a-day workers took either another full-time or a second part-time job. Extra work (or was it just extra money?) was more important to them than increased free time.

The first major qualification of the apparent "leisure revolution" is the difficulty in defining the word *leisure* itself. The issue is complex. What is leisure? How is it related to play? Does it imply idleness or passivity? The questions can go on and on. And in the next chapter we will in fact deal in some detail with the problem of defining terms. But at this juncture two preliminary distinctions are necessary. Francis R. Duffy defines leisure time as "that part of a person's daily life which is not devoted to or absorbed by economic activities. In simple terms it means a period during which one is free from labor."[13] But such a definition needs further qualification. Leisure is not just time free from one's vocation but time free from all *non*-job duties. In this light, eating, sleeping, and shaving are not usually leisure activities, though they can become that (you can eat or shave in a leisurely fashion if you like).

Secondly, leisure is not the inevitable result of spare time or a vacation. As Josef Pieper suggests, "It is, in the first place, *an attitude of mind,* a condition of the soul. . . ."[14] Marion Clawson notes this qualitative distinction regarding leisure by recognizing that within one's discretionary time (what we have called merely "leisure-time"), some activities are what might be labeled "unfun," i.e., "those undertaken out of boredom, or for escape, or because of lack of better opportunities."[15] Other activities are undertaken positively and "in fun" because one wants and enjoys them. The term *leisure* (and the use of other related words yet to be defined, e.g., *play, festivity, games,* etc.) might best be limited to refer only to Clawson's "fun activities," with a more neutral term such as *discretionary time* being used to indicate those moments or hours free from subsistence activity.

A further qualification, one already alluded to, emerges from the above discussion. Because leisure involves one's attitude, leisure that is coerced or enforced is not really leisure at all. As Charles Brightbill observes in *Education for Leisure-Centered Living,* "Real leisure is never imposed. . . . It is the time we use to rest, reflect, meditate, or enjoy a creative or recreative experience."[16] During the Depression in America, for example, the word *leisure* was not popular. It was too often equated with unemployment and implied frustrating hours to seek new employment, days to reflect on failed dreams, and time to worry over one's family and its future security. From this historical vantage point, we can perhaps understand Ralph Abernathy's observations:

> It is a misnomer to think that poor people have leisure time. Their total existence is for survival. . . . While poor people do have their moments of escape from the reality of being poor, their escape pattern usually turns toward the continuous attempt to break out of the trap of despairing poverty.
>
> . . . .
>
> There is no leisure time for poor people. It is difficult to have a leisurely existence when you are unemployed, when you see your children sick, when you live in rat-infested homes and when you see the administration taking careless attitudes toward your plight. Many poor escape this kind of existence for whatever solace can be found in the whiskey bottle and in hard drugs. But they know— all of us know—that is not leisure.[17]

To have leisure time, the larger concerns of life must be temporarily suspended. If issues of survival, or even of mortality, intrude, one's leisure experience is aborted.

Thirdly, any discussion of the increase in leisure time in America must note the counter-trend of women moving prominently into the paid work force. The traditional ethic of women staying in the home is crumbling. Despite continuing low pay and high concentrations of women in certain "feminine" occupations, many women are opting to work in the marketplace. As Daniel Yankelovich points out, "By the late seventies a majority of women (51 percent) were working outside the home. By 1980, more than two out of five mothers of children age six or younger worked for pay. In families earning more than $25,000 a year, the majority now depend on two incomes: the husband's and the wife's."[18] Given the fact that these same women still dominate that major field of unpaid work—homemaking—and are most often perceived as primarily responsible for child-rearing, there exists an increasing number of Americans who have decided, whether because of economic necessity, personal goals, or a desire to break free of sexual stereotyping, to have less leisure time.[19]

Fourth, many have thought that discussion of leisure should center on what to do with our free time and how to make it meaningful. Staffan Linder takes an opposite tack, believing that the leisure problem can be understood by taking into account the fact that "the pace [of life] is quickening, and our lives in fact are becoming steadily more hectic." We have committed ourselves as a nation and as individuals to working for a still higher economic growth rate. In the process, we have forgotten that time is a "scarce commodity." As Linder says, "It is important to realize that consumption requires time just as production. Such pleasures as a cup of coffee or a good stage play are not in fact pleasurable unless we can devote time to enjoying them."[20]

Linder suggests that traditional pleasures, such as eating and contemplation and sex, will be given increasingly little time in the future as consumption time squeezes them out. Thus, although our age is characterized by its sexual orientation, Linder provocatively suggests that we are actually "devoting less and less time to it":

> People have not stopped making love any more than they have stopped eating. But — to extend the surprisingly adequate parallel with the joys of gastronomy — less time is devoted to both preparation and savoring. As a result, we get an increasing amount of frozen nutrition at rapid sittings — the time, on occasion, being too short for any effort to be made at all at stilling the hunger. A pleasure has been turned into the satisfaction of a basic need — "a grocer's orgy" — a maintenance function — a conjugal duty.[21]

Many Americans have joined "the harried leisure class" (this phrase is the title of Linder's book). In the process they have turned the possibility of leisure time into a problematic issue.

Fifth, the increasingly strong push toward "leisure" in America is largely the product of the needs of industrial life. Consumption is replacing production as the central organizing principle of the economy, and thus industry has found it necessary to create a larger and larger leisure market. Most men who retire, for example, do so not because they desire increased leisure time but because industry dictates it. A study of persons drawing Social Security benefits showed that only seventeen percent of those retiring in good health said they did so to enjoy leisure.[22] Even before retirement, "leisure" is increasingly necessary to business. Business executives take up golf because it gives them good opportunities to pursue business relations. Large corporations promote all sorts of sports activities, musical groups, and theatre productions, not primarily because these provide opportunities for leisure but because of their cash value for the business. As the head of employee relations at General Motors said, "Many of these off-the-job or after-hours activities have not only a therapeutic value, but can actually sharpen or increase employees' skills."[23] In other words, leisure-time pursuits are often encouraged for distinctly non-leisure ends. The frequent result is that participants lose the attitude necessary for true leisure.

A sixth and final qualification of the "leisure revolution" is this: what time Americans do spend away from their jobs is often best described as idleness. True, we cannot prove this observation strictly from what Americans do not do in their free time. But its validity was suggested as early as 1969, when a Gallup Poll revealed that 58 percent of all Americans had never finished reading a book other than a textbook or the Bible, and only 26 percent had read a book in the previous month.[24] One reason for this near-illiteracy is America's addiction to television. The average American in 1981 watched over six hours of television a day. Moreover, in order to stimulate these idle viewers, programs have made sex and violence the staples of the television diet — along with instant replays to show us what we miss in our semi-stupor and Howard Cosell to titillate us with locker-room gossip. This inertia has some just cause, as Staffan Linder points out: "The mental energy and internal concentration required to cultivate the mind and spirit adequately are not easily mobilized after a hectic day. When one goes to a concert [or reads a book or even watches television] to relax after a busy day, the result can be a mild drowsiness — in itself pleasurable enough — rather than any spiritual uplift."[25] The personal effort needed to play adequately, even as a spectator, is not easily made after a busy day or week.

Although the amount of discretionary time available to the average American continues to grow every year, Americans are having difficulty learning, as a society, how to play meaningfully. Some are clamoring for recognition in the marketplace, others are frenetically seeking out every new leisure fad. (Video arcades were a five-billion-dollar industry in 1981.) And when we can no longer jog, or we need to escape, the ever-present television set provides us hours of mindless companionship. What is wrong? Why is the increased time for leisure in contemporary America "a problem rather than a collective celebration"?[26] Why is it that with the *potential* for play increasing, and the *need* for play present, our *practice* of play remains so questionable?

I agree with the growing number of critics who suggest that what is wrong is our continuing attitude as a people. We have yet to understand the value or significance of our play. Rather than viewing it as an opportunity, a cause for celebration, most of us consider our increased leisure a threat. As Lawrence Greenberger notes, ". . . mentally and emotionally we have not fully accepted our new leisure for what it is — an opportunity to do and enjoy, a chance to realize the full benefits to be derived from the leisure we now have and will have in even greater abundance."[27]

The sources of our current unrest are certainly many, but if we oversimplify somewhat we can reduce them to two: (1) America's present inability to escape her compulsion about work, and (2) the continuing distorted value structure that has developed in our contemporary technopolis.[28] These are the chief roadblocks confronting the individual (whether Christian or not) who would seek to play authentically. They also constitute the backdrop against which our further discussion of a theology of play must be viewed.

The Leisure Problem: A Matter of Attitude

1. "The Devil Finds Work for Idle Hands"

I regard the five-day week as an unworthy ideal . . . more work and better work is a more inspiring and worthier motto than less work and more pay. . . . It is better not to trifle or tamper with God's laws.

—JOHN E. EDGERTON,
President, National Association of Manufacturers (1926)[29]

For Mr. Edgerton, work was not a part of life but life itself. It was the way of progress and prosperity — yea, of God himself! To a lesser degree, this has been the prevalent stance in America, and still is today. In his humorous but pointed book *Confessions of a Workaholic,* Wayne Oates has summarized much of our modern belief in these words: "The workaholic's way of life is considered in America to be at one and the same time (a) a religious virtue, (b) a form of patriotism, (c) the way to win friends and influence people, and (d) the way to be healthy, wealthy, and wise."[30] Hard work with sufficient time off for diversion and recreation has been and remains in America the basic formula for a meaningful life. There is some difference of opinion, however, about the basis for this belief. Some, taking their cue from Max Weber and R. H. Tawney, see our work ethic as stemming from our Puritan background.[31] Others have found its basis in the pragmatic and competitive philosophy of secular America. Neither explanation excludes the other. In fact, it can be demonstrated that they are opposite sides of the same coin: both our Protestant and our competitive world-views support our continuing obsession with work.

The Puritan, or Protestant, work ethic has certainly played a prominent role in American life. Benjamin Franklin's *Poor Richard's Almanac* and "The Village Blacksmith" by Longfellow are but two of countless indications of its pervasiveness. An even better example is John Wesley's "Money Sermon," in which he preached that one should earn all he can, save all he can, and give all he can. Ministers in Methodist churches across the nation echoed these words for generations. The glorification of work as a calling of God, the belief that success can be equated with meaningfulness in life, the universal prohibition against idleness, the drive toward activity, industry, frugality, and efficiency as religious ideals, the belief that poverty is a sign of sin, and the emphasis on self-discipline and individualism—all became part of the American ethos. And while the religious foundations for such an orientation are crumbling, the ethical superstructure has remained. Thus Canadian journalist Pierre Berton argues in his book *The Smug Minority* that "a mystical belief in the value of work still has a firm hold upon the cultural unconscious of North American society. Work seems to be the one thoroughly acceptable way that a man can demonstrate his worth to himself and his peers."[32]

Such an evaluation is today being challenged in some quarters, but industry, individualism, frugality, ambition, and success are still considered primary virtues by the majority of Americans. (A case in point is Richard Nixon's Labor Day Message, September 6, 1971: "Let the detractors of America, the doubters of the American spirit, take note. America's competitive spirit, the work-ethic of this people, is alive and well on Labor Day, 1971. The dignity of work, the value of achievement, the morality of self-reliance—none of these is going out of style."[33]) Arnold Green has noted that the Protestant ethic can and will continue to wane in America *without* being accompanied by a weakening of the work effort, i.e., of the superstructure.[34] It is this corpse—the spiritless remains of the Protestant work ethic—that largely explains the modern worker's attempt to overcome the lack of quality and meaning in his work by substituting increased quantities of work time. Even potentially non-work situations are given their *raison d'etre* by being brought under the work umbrella. Thus we justify our reading as "homework" and our exercise as "working out." Like the Puritans, most of us still consider work to be the criterion by which a life is judged successful or unsuccessful. As the Congressional study *Work in America* concludes: "Doing well or poorly, being a success or failure at work, is all too easily transformed into a measure of being a valuable or worthless human being. . . ."[35] This is the work ethic.

Other critics have attempted to explain America's preoccupation with work as a reflection of her basic pragmatic, or utilitarian, outlook. In *The Decline of Pleasure,* Walter Kerr takes this tack. He criticizes those who say we are haunted by a Puritan mentality. We abandoned Puritanism long ago, he claims. We twentieth-century Americans work because it is *useful* for us to do so. By working we get more money, and thus more opportunities for pleasure and happiness. But this drive carries over: we feel that even those activities that provide no financial remuneration must be useful. Thus, Kerr says,

> We are all of us compelled to read for profit, party for contacts, lunch for contracts, bowl for unity, drive for mileage, gamble for charity, go out for the evening for the greater glory of the municipality, and stay home for the weekend to rebuild the house. . . . In a contrary and perhaps rather cruel way the twentieth cen-

tury has relieved us of labor without at the same time relieving us of the conviction that only labor is meaningful.[36]

Eric Hoffer would argue that it is not utilitarianism so much as America's penchant for activity that lies behind her preoccupation with work. He says, "The superficiality of the American is the result of his hustling . . . people in a hurry cannot think, cannot grow nor can they decay. They are preserved in a state of perpetual puerility."[37] According to Hoffer, we work in order to remain occupied. We cannot as a people endure life's pauses.

While both Kerr and Hoffer have recognized important aspects of America's national character, their insights seem to be helpful primarily in indicating two facets of a more basic drive that motivates the modern American. This primal force, I would submit, is America's commitment to a competitive spirit. We do everything possible to "win," both as individuals and as a people. And the pursuit of success too often enslaves us. Competition is the reason behind much of our otherwise random activity and is the basic criterion by which we choose what is useful. If this thesis can be maintained, what we have is a secularized version of the Protestant ethic—one that glorifies success, preaches sacrifice in order to get ahead, understands work as a "calling," and emphasizes individualism.

David Potter has perhaps most forcefully argued that the competitive spirit has been the major determinant of America's national character. In his book *People of Plenty,* he analyzes the writings of Margaret Mead, David Riesman, and Karen Horney. All three have attempted to show within their own disciplines that uniformities of attitude and behavior in America do exist. Potter concludes:

> Drawing these three interpretations together, then, we have three treatments which agree, or may be construed as agreeing, that the American character is in a large measure a group of responses to an unusually competitive situation. Competition may be factored out time and again as a common denominator. . . . [38]

Potter would not necessarily agree with me that competition is but the secular version of the Protestant work ethic. He would posit economic abundance as the causal agent of competition. While not denying the impetus that abundance gives to the spirit of competition, I think it is more enlightening in this context to stress the similarity of focus in both the religious and the secular versions of America's national character. In both instances, work becomes a primary means of evaluating success and worthwhileness.

In his recent book, *New Rules: Searching for Self-Fulfillment in a World Turned Upside Down,* Daniel Yankelovich documents an apparent shift by some Americans away from a work mentality: ". . . far fewer Americans now than in 1970 judge their own fulfillment in life by the standards of competitive success."[39] Some, that is, have abandoned their commitment to the traditional work ethic. A variety of reasons might be given to explain this shift, but the chief one, according to Yankelovich, is the fact that many people have achieved the work goals of previous generations and yet have not experienced the self-fulfillment they thought would follow. This has produced a growing suspicion among the young. After "almost thirty years of the greatest prosperity the world has ever known," after an extended period when hard work and sacrifice have paid off and when private goals have resonated with public virtues, there has been a shift inward, especially among the younger, better-educated members of the population. The old ethic of self-denial has been turned upside-down. "Creativity," rather than competition, has become the hallmark of their life-style. Yankelovich documents the fact that for seventeen percent of all Americans the search for self-fulfillment has become an obsession.

Do these people who follow a set of "new rules" qualify the claim that America remains obsessed with work? Are these more "creative" types the harbingers of a new age? Yes and no. Although a work mentality might, at first glance, seem to be missing among this growing counterculture, on closer inspection it proves to be alive and well, albeit in disguise. Yankelovich labels those who follow the new rules "strong formers." His conclusion is this:

> Strong formers stand squarely in the mainstream of the traditional American pursuit of self-improvement. Only when it comes to the *object* of self-improvement do they veer sharply from tradition. In the past the purpose of self-improvement was to better oneself in the tangible, visible ways associated with worldly or familial suc-

cess. But for these strong formers the object of their creative energies is . . . themselves.[40]

The seeming shift away from a competitive work ethic has been in reality merely a turning toward a new work object. In the words of Christopher Lasch, "the culture of competitive individualism with its focus on external achievement has been replaced by *The Culture of Narcissism* with its focus on internal accomplishment."[41] Or, to use Yankelovich's words, what we observe is "a nonrebel in rebel's clothing."[42] Those in the growing counterculture remain work-oriented; now, however, their goal is their own self-fulfillment. Self-help endeavors abound among this group: 43 percent join encounter groups, 48 percent meditate, 57 percent analyze their dreams, 34 percent would like to belong to a literary discussion group, 50 percent prefer health food, 71 percent exercise, and 27 percent eat yogurt. All of these percentages are significantly above the national norm. In all of this, Yankelovich says,

> the continuity with the past is inescapable. The classic American theme of self-improvement stands out prominently, as does faith in education, and an evangelical streak of earnestness that runs throughout the American saga. . . . What is new is the shift in the object of all this energy, a shift from the external to the inner world.[43]

Regardless of whether it is framed in its religious or its secular context, regardless of whether the object of one's energy is external or internal, America's understanding of her national character continues to place work at the forefront. All other aspects of life tend to be formed and defined by their relationship to work. Here is the key to understanding leisure (play) in much of contemporary American life. Leisure is not viewed as an independent occurrence, or even a complementary activity. Rather, it is placed under the tyranny of a work mentality. It is indeed a tyranny, for viewing leisure with a basic work orientation results in an unfortunate diminishment of the leisure experience.

In American society, leisure has been reduced to what Walter Kerr calls an "incidental delight":

> We are in the market—and a very limited market it is—for lazy delight, for incidental delight, for delight that need be only half

attended to, for the fruits of the imagination made easy and un-obtrusive. We insist that our pleasures be unobtrusive because we have no intention whatever of withdrawing our attention from our proper goals, from the profits to be taken from respectable em-ployment. We do not mean to work for a while and then play for a while. We mean to work all of the time and let play come to us in passing, like a sandwich that is brought to the desk.[44]

Thus television scripts must be written so that if the viewer is distracted by the need to answer the doorbell or perform some other chore, he will be able to pick up the plot of the program without difficulty on his return. Soap operas are perhaps the epitome of this phenomenon; viewers need to watch the serial only every other day or so to know all that transpires. Similarly, novels must be written so that they may be easily picked up or put down. They become the "small pleasures" we allow our-selves in our free time. Even Monday-night football becomes mere packaged entertainment, the drama of the game being sub-merged in a welter of personal interviews, sociological commen-tary, and mindless banter.

At worst such leisure becomes a great emptiness—a time void of any meaningful activity. At best it serves to fill in the blank spaces of a life of permanent busy-ness by providing spo-radic excitations and diversions. But that which should be an extension of personal freedom becomes for most a mechanized response, one that escapes idleness but that has been so routin-ized by mass conformity to current moods and fads that its personal expressiveness has been lost.

It is my conviction that America's continued belief in a work-dominated value system has obscured her vision of life's possibilities. It has made it impossible for her to accept cre-atively the increased opportunity for leisure (play) which a grow-ing amount of discretionary time provides. A little leisure time is quite acceptable, and the vice of idleness is not really even a "major sin" if kept in manageable (dare I say workable?) pro-portions. But too much free time without the opportunity for work is a threat to one's being. I am reminded here of the com-ment of a high-school football coach from Durham, North Car-olina; when interviewed by a newspaper reporter, he compared his impending retirement with an automobile accident: "You always think of an accident happening to someone else but not to you."[45] To this coach, the prospect of an increase in discretionary time was an unattractive one—one to be avoided if at all possible. The problem facing American society is this: it is increasingly difficult to avoid the "accident" of free time that cannot be justified within an individual's work-oriented world. Could it be that what is needed is an alternate attitude toward life, a different pattern of meaning by which to view the world, a new master image for human beings, a new theological orientation, one that would allow work its rightful place while at the same time finding intrinsic value in leisure and play?

2. Our Current Dis-ease: "Men Without Chests"

"The trouble of the modern age," writes T.S. Eliot in On Poetry and Poets, *"is not . . . the inability to believe certain things about God and man which our forefathers believed." Indeed, some of our assumptions are just as preposterous and superstitious, just as irrational and absurd. But the trouble is "the inability to* feel *towards God and man as they did."*

—GABRIEL VAHANIAN[46]

I'd rather learn from one bird how to sing than teach ten thousand stars how not to dance.
—E. E. CUMMINGS[47]

There is, in addition to our "workaholism," a second major factor contributing to the problem of leisure. If sociologists have tended to center on the foregoing argument and to single out work as the basis of their assessment of our present inability to play authentically, theologians and philosophers have tended to focus upon a second area: America's distorted value structure that has accepted as true the "mindscape" of technology.[48] This is Theodore Roszak's phrase, and his discussion can perhaps serve as a helpful starting point.

Roszak, in his book *Where the Wasteland Ends: Politics and Transcendence in Post-Industrial Society,* argues that the "mindscape" by which our culture has been shaped over the past three centuries is a false and limited one. Having developed alongside modern science, this attitude toward the world cannot be equated merely with what people "objectively" know or say they believe. "What matters is something deeper: the feel of the world around us, the sense of reality, the taste that spontaneously discriminates between knowledge and fantasy."[49] Although most of our society, at the popular level, is scientifically illiterate, we have accepted a scientific world-view as our paradigm. We have come to believe with Buckminster Fuller that it is upon inventing the machine that "man . . . began for the first time to really employ his intellect in the most important way."[50]

Roszak believes the ideal of scientific objectivity has created a narrowing of our sensibilities, a diminished mode of consciousness. It is a "single vision" (the phrase is borrowed from William Blake) that can measure only a portion of what one can know. As Roszak states:

> Yet my contention is that the universe of single vision, the orthodox consciousness in which most of us reside most of the time and especially when we are being most "wide awake" and "realistic," is very cramped quarters, by no means various and spacious enough to let us grow to full human size.

That we have narrowed sensibilities can be illustrated in many ways, suggests Roszak. We repress our dreams; it requires painfully bright lights to hurt our eyes and startlingly loud sounds to pierce our ears (one need only recall the light-and-sound shows of rock performers); and most of us take up exclusive residence in our heads, repressing our bodies. (I am reminded of a young woman I observed who, when asked by Sam Keen to draw a picture of herself, drew only her head and a pair of stick legs.) All of these are indicators of our personal alienation—our common disease. "Taken together," Roszak says, "they describe the major contours of the psychic wasteland we carry within us as we make our way through the 'real' world of the artificial environment." Roszak recalls how Augustine described idolatry: " 'Mankind tyrannized over by the work of his own hands.' "[51]

Roszak does not want to deny that science has any value. He only wants to challenge science's claim of providing "our *only* reliable access to reality," and to keep "first things first," i.e., to put the human first. For Roszak, a "culture based on [such] single vision is dehumanizing." Life has been robotized.

"The well-focused eye may see sharply what it sees, but it studies a lesser reality than the enraptured gaze."[52] The task of science is to increase what is known—to accumulate facts, refine its methods of observation, and render its body of theory ever more abstract. Its intent is neither to deepen the personality of the knower nor to enhance the charm, autonomy, dignity, and mystery of the known. As Kathleen Raine puts it, our culture's dominant mindscape would have us "see in the pearl nothing but a disease of the oyster."[53]

Roszak is hardly a lone voice crying in the wilderness. He is one of a chorus of critics whose expertise ranges across the academic disciplines—philosophers, geologists, drama critics, literary men and women, students of law and of history, theologians, and so on. It is impossible to survey adequately this multi-disciplinary reaction to our "single-visioned" mindscape, but perhaps I can capture its spirit and breadth in what follows.

Gabriel Marcel, the French "neo-Socratic" philosopher, has said, "The dynamic element in my philosophy, taken as a whole, can be seen as an obstinate and untiring battle against the spirit of abstraction."[54] Like Roszak, Marcel is not opposed to all abstraction, which is, after all, basic to thought and consistent action. Rather, he dwells on the adverse effects of the *spirit* of abstraction—that imperialistic fascination which betrays the concrete reality itself. In his book *Being and Having,* Marcel uses a series of polarities to delineate two basic modes of relating to the world: being and having; participation and objectification; mystery and problem; presence and object; I-Thou relationships and I-It relationships; thought which stands in the presence of, and thought which proceeds by interrogation; concrete thinking and abstraction; secondary reflection and primary reflection.[55] Marcel recognizes that both modes of relating to the world are necessary, but he feels the contemporary person is increasingly becoming a slave to the possessive orientation. Because of this our human spirit is in danger—it suffers "disease."

Martin Heidegger's view is similar to that of Marcel on this point. He believes that our penchant in the West for "calculative thinking" has caused us to miss Being. We cannot approach the world as a project to be tackled but only in the spirit of what Heidegger calls *Gelassenheit* (surrender, acquiescence). Only then will the voice of Being be heard. James M. Houston, an Oxford geologist for twenty years and a lay theologian, in an article entitled "The Loss and Recovery of the Personal," also questions "the all sufficiency of the technologist's empiricism and the intellectual posture of scientism." He believes "to avert the theory-centered and egocentric predicament of man, we must turn from the definition of man, 'I think, therefore I am,' to the action-oriented stance, 'I respond, therefore I am.' "[56] Echoing Jacques Ellul, he says,

> [Our society is] completely orientated toward technique as the instrument of performance, of power, of man's worship.
>
> . . . .
>
> So far has this worship, or what we may call "technolatry," gone that there is a deep conviction that technical problems are the only serious problems of society, so that public opinion, the social structure and the state are all oriented towards technology. In consequence, man no longer has any means by which to subjugate technique to himself; rather he is demeaned so that man is subservient to technology. Man tends no longer to be a person; rather he is appraised by the techniques he represents in his training, as a scientist, philosopher, artist, mechanic, or typist.[57]

Those who study the arts register similar evaluations of our modern mindscape. Walter Kerr, a drama critic who speaks out of a direct interest in the play experience, bemoans the fact that when children today are given a choice between a road map and *Robinson Crusoe*, they will often choose the road map. The contemporary child, he feels, is a "factgatherer." "He does not long for greener, gayer hills. He is happy that his view of the universe is less 'distorted' than mine was, and is; happy that he knows more about the moon and pterodactyls than I do."[58] Literary critic Walter Ong makes a similar complaint: "It is no accident that the most strenuous corporate technological effort which man has ever made coincides *in fact* with the activity which earlier man often *jokingly* imagined to be the most playful . . . shooting the moon."[59]

One can multiply such witnesses to our present situation. At this point it is perhaps necessary only to note that such criticism of modern America's mistaken value structure has not escaped her theologians. Thus Frederick Herzog in his *Libera-*

tion Theology states categorically, *"Our image of man must go"* (italics his).[60] He thinks that our present image, which is a fusion of the Puritan and the Cartesian, needs to be confronted by Jesus, who offers every person a new self. We need, says Herzog, to turn from the private, modern self to the corporate self.

Harvey Cox, the theological popularizer and prophet who wrote *The Secular City* in 1965 in celebration of the new freedom given to us by secularization and urbanization, has since that time shifted his emphasis to deploring the threat of technological imperialism.[61] He believes that technology and its artifacts currently "release emotions incommensurate with their mere utility," i.e., they "arouse hopes and fears only indirectly related to their use." In short, technologies are becoming religious symbols and are in the process of destroying the cultural and anthropological balance between energy and form, spirit and structure. Religion must seek to restore the balance, Cox believes, by being partisan toward the playful. "We have contracted the cultural and religious equivalent of leukemia. In leukemia, the balance between white and red blood cells is lost. The white cells first outnumber, then begin to cannibalize the red ones. In time the victim invariably dies."[62]

Much of current scholarship renders the same diagnosis of our contemporary "dis-ease." The inroad into the discussion is very often dependent upon the academic discipline in which the critic has expertise, but the overall shape of the argument is similar across disciplines. There is, first of all, a recognition of the overweening influence and authority of scientism and its outward manifestation, technocracy. The contemporary Western person has falsely valued objectivity, refusing to recognize that it is in reality what Rubem Alves calls the logic of "the dinosaur," threatening the ongoing vitality of life.[63]

Secondly, as Wesley Kort summarizes, our present conceptual system "is a system based on the ruthless exclusion of the personal, a systematic skepticism which renders the 'I' an eye measuring mathematically the relations to one another of phenomena in the objective world."[64] Such depersonalism necessarily carries with it a denial of the person's full humanness. As Harvey Cox states:

> The tight, bureaucratic and industrial society—the only model we've known since the industrial revolution—renders us incapable

of experiencing the nonrational dimensions of existence. The absurd, the inspiring, the uncanny, the awesome, the terrifying, the ecstatic—none of these fits into a production- and efficiency-oriented society.[65]

Self-enclosed in a tiny, windowless universe, the individual mistakenly assumes his creation to be the only possible one. The result is, in C. S. Lewis's phrase, "the abolition of man."[66]

Thirdly, recognizing our grave situation, many critics of American society have nevertheless realized that there is no going back. Although technological thinking must be challenged, a romantic escape to a pre-industrial age will not do. Not everyone has avoided this trap; theologians of play seem particularly susceptible to it, as we will observe in Chapter Four. It is nonetheless helpful to assert here the importance of avoiding both an a-historicism that would fail to take our contemporary context seriously and a truncated anthropology that would escape one danger to our humanness (a denial of the spontaneous, the individual, the free) by fleeing to another (a denial of order, community, destiny).

Lastly, while recognizing the need to take our present context seriously, we must also realize, as Rubem Alves does, that we need "a fresh start."[67] Our basic attitude toward life—our master image by which we have attempted to integrate life's various facets, our stance toward reality, our metaphor of contemporary meaning, our paradigm by which to view the world, our world view, or mindscape (one can pick the expression that best suits his or her interests and/or academic discipline, for these terms are all roughly equivalent)—is in need of reworking. As Alves has declared, we need "a new paradigm for understanding the conditions of human life. In the beautiful phrase of Paul Lehmann, our problem is to find out 'what it takes to make and to keep human life human in the world.' "[68]

It is this goal that has led most of the critics mentioned here to explore the possible relevance and importance of play as an antidote for our technological dis-ease. They have asked what there is of human value in play—"play" both as the experience itself and as a possible master image for making and keeping human life human. Thus Herzog and Heidegger both believe we must become poets; Alves sees the creative imagination as the key to our rebirth; and Roszak argues romantically for the visionary and rhapsodic.

Whether we look at the dislocation of our leisure caused by a continuing compulsion about work, or whether we focus upon the loss of the fully personal to the imperialism of a single-visioned mindscape, we are led to entertain the possibilities that human life is larger than currently conceived, and that the experience and concept of play might provide the contemporary person with a way into these larger realities. As a Christian church, we are being addressed on these issues by our surrounding culture. Our concept of the image of "man" is being challenged. Moreover, we are being told that play is a possible way out of our cultural and spiritual malaise. This book is directed to the question, How can we understand this new impulse theologically? What can we as a Christian church learn from these cultural prophets? And what, if anything, can Christian theology, from its own unique position, offer in return?

II
Play:
A Matter of Definition

UP TO THIS POINT, WE HAVE AVOIDED MOST MATTERS dealing with definition in order to first become acquainted with the possibilities and problems facing the player today. But questions of definition cannot be ignored if we are to have a meaningful discussion, even if answers are not readily forthcoming. As George Sheehan, a practicing cardiologist and the best-selling author of *On Running,* comments: "Perhaps even more difficult than discovering play is defining it."[1] Some of the confusion about play stems from ambiguities surrounding the use of the term *play* itself. The *Random House Dictionary* lists fifty-three meanings of *play,* not counting such idioms as "He made a play for my girl."[2] The play of the wind, playing a role, playing an instrument, playing house, and love play only scratch the surface. Complicating the picture still further is the use of *play* to describe such non-play situations as the strategies of business, diplomacy, and war—"a range of activities," as Richard Burke suggests, "about as far from play as one can imagine."[3] But our inability to define play clearly cannot be blamed on its extended usage or its misuse. The fundamental problem lies within play itself: to quote George Sheehan again, ". . . play is an attitude as well as an action."[4]

Is the tense businessman who takes out his frustrations on the tennis court a player, while the independently wealthy and carefree tennis player who turns professional is a worker? Probably not. But there is no clear-cut means available to make a decision without attempting an assessment of the varying and imprecise attitudes involved. A description of one's activity alone is insufficient to determine whether it is play. Exceptions for every "objective" standard can always be found. Games are play, for example, except for the coach of the team (usually) and perhaps for those who feel an overwhelming need to win. Plays are play, as Walter Ong observes, except for the playwright and perhaps some of the paying public.[5] Moreover, while most would say that tennis and drama provide at least the occasion for play (even if some tennis players, for example, are not actually "playing"), the list of possible play activities is much broader than we often imagine, including much of life — more, in any case, than just tennis, reading, dancing, etc. *Tom Sawyer* provides a well-known example. Recall that when Tom's aunt ordered him to paint the fence, Tom complained about the task. But when Tom fooled the other boys into thinking it was play, they even brought him their jackknives and tops for the "privilege" of painting a few boards. For his friends, fence-painting was play; for Tom, it was hard work.

In his seminal book on play, *Homo Ludens,* cultural historian Johan Huizinga states, "Play is a function of the living, but it is not susceptible of exact definition either logically, biologically, or aesthetically."[6] Like the definitions of *art* or *love* or *life,* the definition of *play* proves illusive. The best support for Huizinga's hesitancy in attempting a precise definition of play is surely the recognized inadequacy of other efforts made to do so. Those who have defined the meaning of play have consistently been guilty of reducing it to something other than play in its fullness, an error we have already noted in those who would understand play as merely "free time."[7] Others would view play as the discharge of surplus energy (Herbert Spencer, J.C. Friedrich von Schiller); or alternately as relaxation, as recuperation from exhaustion (G. T. W. Patrick, Moritz Lazarus). Play is sometimes viewed as an instinct educator (Karl Groos); as a means of catharsis, a safety valve to vent emotions (Aristotle); as a creative modeling of situations that enables the player to better handle experience (Erik Erikson); as a means of resolving psychic conflict (Sigmund Freud), or, on the contrary, as activity *not* motivated by the need to resolve inner conflict (Robert Neale).[8]

Rather than proceed with such definitions, it will prove more useful if we seek only to describe some of play's common features, attitudes, and consequences. These will provide a clear basis for commentary on the Christian value of such "play."

The Characteristics of Play

Real singing is a different breath. A breath for
nothing. A wafting in a god. A wind.
                    —RAINER MARIA RILKE[9]

Johan Huizinga's *Homo Ludens* contains the most widely used description of play:

> Summing up the formal characteristics of play we might call it a free activity standing quite consciously outside "ordinary" life as being "not serious," but at the same time absorbing the player intensely and utterly. It is an activity connected with no material interest, and no profit can be gained by it. It proceeds within its own proper boundaries of time and space according to fixed rules and in an orderly manner. It promotes the formation of social groupings which tend to surround themselves with secrecy and to stress their difference from the common world by disguises or other means.[10]

Countless other descriptions have been offered, however. Richard Burke, an Oakland University philosopher, discusses play in this way:

> (A) few common features emerge: freedom from compulsion, completeness of the activity itself apart from its result, and a certain artificial or "pretend" quality which is unobservable and hard to pin down but which is nevertheless present, I think, in the organized games and performances of adults, and even in the random exuberance of the child. I would define "play," therefore, as *activity which is free, complete in itself, and artificial or unrealistic.* I might add that play is often governed by rules, either explicit (as in game) or implicit (there are rules of impersonation, for example) and that it often involves a test or contest.[11]

Child psychologist Jean Piaget believes that play has two primary features: it is done "for the pleasure of the activity [something Burke and Huizinga ignore] and without any effort at adaptation to achieve a definite end." Piaget believes the attitude of the child is what shows whether or not the child is playing, and he seeks to distinguish between "efforts to learn" and those activities which are "only a happy display of known actions."[12] Robert Neale, Professor of Theology and Psychology at Union Seminary, agrees that attitude is crucial, believing play is distinguished by a sense of "adventure" as well as "by those elements of peace, freedom, delight, and illusion that occur in the modes of story and game."[13]

These examples indicate something of the range of thought concerning play. Rather than focus directly upon any one of these observers of play, however, let me venture my own description of it, a description that is informed both by these and by other students of play.

I would understand play as that activity which is freely and spontaneously entered into, but which, once begun, has its own design, its own rules or order, which must be followed so that the play activity may continue. The player is called into play by a potential co-player and/or play object, and while at play, treats other players and/or "playthings" as personal, creating with them a community that can be characterized by "I-Thou" rather than "I-It" relationships. This play has a new time (a playtime) and a new space (a playground) which function as "parentheses" in the life and world of the player. The concerns of everyday life come to a temporary standstill in the mind of the player, and the boundaries of his or her world are redefined. Play, to be play, must be entered into without outside purpose; it cannot be connected with a material interest or ulterior motive, for then the boundaries of the playground and the limits of the playtime are violated. But though play is an end in itself, it can nevertheless have several consequences. Chief among these are the joy and release, the personal fulfillment, the remembering of our common humanity, and the presentiment of the sacred, which the player sometimes experiences in and through the activity. One's participation in the adventure of playing, even given the risk of injury or defeat, finds resolution at the end of the experience, and one re-enters ongoing life in a new spirit of thanksgiving and celebration. The player is a changed individual because of the playtime, his or her life having been enlarged beyond the workaday world.

Of course, a host of issues are related to such a description, issues that will be discussed in due course. What does it mean for an activity to be free? How can solitary play be personal? What of those who begin an activity purposefully but end up playing? Nonetheless, it should be apparent even at this preliminary juncture that the player is one who successfully holds in tension a variety of polarities. In what follows I will elaborate upon this theme along these lines: (1) although players do not escape the everyday world, which remains as a horizon or background to play, they accept a new set of time-and-space boundaries in order to play; (2) although people voluntarily choose to play, they do so in an attitude of receptivity, recognizing that in some sense they have also been invited to play; (3) there is a spontaneity in play (regardless of prior preparation), but never at the expense of play's forms or orderliness; and (4) though play is non-utilitarian—an end in itself—it nevertheless proves productive beyond its own boundaries. Such a description of play emphasizes the attitudes of the participants. Concluding this section on the characteristics of play will be a spelling-out of some of the implications of play's attitudinal locus.

1. Playgrounds and Playtimes

The world of play lives by forgetting.
—RUBEM ALVES[14]

When the game is on between U.S.C. and U.C.L.A., time stops, world problems cease, and attention is riveted on the football field. There is, to be sure, a clock involved, but it has nothing to do with life's ongoing concerns. Similarly, the action occurs in a fixed place, the Los Angeles Coliseum, but the larger issues of city politics are irrelevant. Perhaps the most distinguishing characteristic of play is its new set of time-and-space boundaries. In play the "real" world is left behind; what is ordinarily relevant is momentarily suspended as life comes to a halt. As psychiatrist Jay Rohrlich says, ". . . there is no 'time' in leisure; there is only the 'present'. . . . Workers measure how quickly they achieve the result they desire. . . . What does it matter if you do your gardening or piano playing *fast*?"[15]

That play is a parenthesis in life has long been recognized. Plato, for example, calls the religious holiday an *anapausa,* a breathing spell.[16] We see it in children's play, where a new space and time are set apart for the duration of the play experience—the back yard becoming a jungle or the Western prairie where the Indians and the cowboys are fighting. We see this in sports, where Roger Bannister's comment about his world-record race (he was the first to run the mile in under four minutes) has often been repeated by other runners: "The world seemed to stand still, or did not exist. . . ."[17] And certainly this can be true of the play world of art, which, according to Gerardus Van der Leeuw, is a new "creation, a second world, with its own power."[18] Sadler states:

> In play an individual takes advantage of an opportunity to intensify and personalize his perception, to set the boundaries of his world, to forge an original space-time, a personal world. . . . In play, one constructs his own space, providing himself with a field of freedom in which to experiment with meanings and to establish his identity. . . . Similarly in play one sets his own time, beyond the measurement of clocks and schedules. . . . Play time is not fragmented but whole; it is ecstatic time that opens up to the new.[19]

Play theorists have by and large agreed with Sadler, while recognizing that the issue is more complex than it at first seems. There is an "as-if-ness" to the play world; it is make-believe. This is true even for the young child. Piaget has observed, for example, that the two- to four-year-old child is aware that in a sense his ludic symbols are not real for others, and he makes no serious attempt to persuade the adult that they are. Rather, he calls the adult to suspend judgment and to enter wholeheartedly into his imaginary world.[20] Similarly, the artist, as Roy Harvey Pearce has suggested, calls us to "willingly suspend our ordinary disbelief in . . . imagined situations and accordingly assent to them." We are not to ask whether *Star Wars* could happen or whether Picasso's *Guernica* is realistic. Pearce labels this response "as-if assent."[21]

For the player, questions of "truth" are simply irrelevant. If, for reasons outside the play experience, larger issues intrude, the play world dissolves. It is for this reason that Johan Huizinga understands that play "lies outside morals. In itself it is neither good nor bad."[22] A particularly graphic illustration of this point was the made-for-TV movie *Playing for Time* (1980), a film which raised a touchy question: How could Jewish women musicians play for Nazis in the concentration camps? The answer given in the film by the Jewish conductor is that music is beyond politics. The irony of the film was that Vanessa Redgrave, a sympathizer with the Palestine Liberation Organization, played the lead role of the French-Jewish cabaret singer, Fania Fenelon. Many believed such casting was an insult to the Jewish people, and boycotted the film. They could not agree with the conductor. For others, however, the film transcended such moral questions while it lasted. These viewers sat transfixed as Redgrave gave television one of its great performances.

Surprisingly, the traditional Sunday "blue laws" also illustrate the amorality of play. On the Sunday holiday, certain kinds of recreation were outlawed, and no violence (which necessarily involves the issue of morality) was supposed to be committed, not even by the criminal. Perhaps a more telling example is the standing ovation that was given two basketball players from North Carolina State University during a game of the 1972-73 season. On a technicality they were allowed to play in the game, even though marijuana had been found in their possession. The crowd was not supportive because they favored legalizing marijuana; they simply thought that such questions of ethics were inappropriate to the basketball arena. Here was a cause for rejoicing; the players had returned to strengthen the team.[23]

Along with the issue of morality might be mentioned the related matter of the non-compulsive character of play. Certainly this is implicit, if not explicit, in the preceding discussion. There should be no profit or material interest motivating the player, nor should play be seen as an attempt to resolve the conflict. This is the basic weakness of psychoanalytical theories of play, which are based on the premise that play compensates for the presence of conflict and releases tension. J. Bernard Gilmore's study of children at play has contradicted the popular notion that play is primarily a form of escape. He found that although seriously frustrated children are looking for ways to escape, they nevertheless demonstrate a significantly diminished capacity to play. For the same reasons, players who feel compelled to cheat dissolve their play worlds by bringing to bear issues from beyond the boundaries of their playground. If, for example, a player needs to have the dice turn up on a certain number and manipulates them to make that happen, he is "working" at his play. The cheater, even in solitaire, knows his play is inauthentic — untrue to the play experience and to life itself.[24]

2. Individual Freedom and Loving Community

Freedom does not die in love;
it is born there.
                                        —WILLIAM SADLER[25]

One must choose to play. He or she must turn aside from the confinements of ordinary concerns, the tensions of the workaday world, and affirm a different order of existence. Our present concept of *Homo Faber* ("Man, the Worker") has, as we have seen, inhibited this exercise of freedom, causing men and women to turn potentially playful experiences into attempts to escape tension, boredom, or fatigue, or into exercises geared at accomplishing something constructive. In the process, the "worker" has been unable to become a "player." Today we are beginning to reassert our awareness that enforced play is never authentic; voluntary consent and self-expression are basic to the play experience. J. C. Friedrich von Schiller's *On the Aesthetic Education of Man* is a still-helpful, albeit extravagant, reading on the relation of play and freedom:

> In the midst of the awful realm of powers, and of the sacred realm of laws, the aesthetic creative impulse is building unawares a third joyous realm of play and of appearance, in which it releases mankind from all the shackles of circumstance and frees him from everything that may be called constraint, whether physical or moral. . . . *To grant freedom by means of freedom* is the fundamental law of this kingdom.[26]

The phrase "to grant freedom by means of freedom" is suggestive, for it implies that the freedom of play is not merely a "freedom *from*" but a "freedom *for.*" Gabriel Vahanian believes that most leisure specialists have made the mistake of contenting themselves with asserting only the last half of this equation — the "freedom from." In the process they have largely ignored that "freedom for" which would convert liberty to liberation and innocence to responsibility.[27]

The move from liberty to liberation and from innocence to responsibility is a complex one. It involves a person in the recognition that freedom is an expression not only of individuality but of community as well. Michelangelo recognized this aspect of play. He stated: "The best of artists never make a creation that is not hid already in the stone, in marble fixed, and yet the work is done by hand, which follows mind and meditation."[28] The artist exercises his craft freely, without constraint, but always in harmony with what the stone calls forth.

There are parallels to Michelangelo's idea in Walter Ong's discussion of belief in literature. Ong distinguishes between belief as opinion (belief "that," which remains egocentric) and belief as faith (belief "in," which involves the reader in an "I-Thou" relationship). He suggests that the latter category is expressive of the communal nature of the literary experience. Literature does not communicate; it communes. Similarly, a reader of a novel or a poem does not analyze; he or she participates. For Ong, the essence of the literary experience is not the compiling of objects and facts (i.e., not the chiseling of a stone) but the interaction of invitation and response, truth being contained in the relationship.[29]

The interactive process that Ong describes regarding the reading of literature is true of the play experience more generally. The boy who is throwing the football through the inner tube is "talking" to the football — recognizing in it a "personal" presence. The lovers in bed who seek to fulfill their play experience do so through a process of give-and-take, each offering the other the full integrity of his or her personhood. Without such interaction the experience is called rape.

The player must exist in concord with his or her co-players and play world. As Walter Kerr says,

> Suppose, in a kind of contented abstinence, we were to refrain from trying to understand more of the landscape before us than the landscape cared to display for us, that we were willing to follow the bend of bough and straggle of gravel and tilt of pole wherever the bend and the straggle and the tilt chanced to take us, that we concerned ourselves not with pattern or profit or even pleasure but merely with watching like a token sentinel in safe country, that we gave our eyes a quiet carte blanche and permitted our minds to play at liberty over the face of an untouched terrain? Could that, then, be called the play of the mind?[30]

In play there is a widening of the field of vision so that the player "sees" life as it presents itself. Such receptivity, characteristic of all forms of play, has been described in many ways. The player has what Goethe calls a "passive attentiveness," what Maslow has labeled "fusion knowledge," or a "caring objectivity." Buber's "name-tag" is perhaps better known — the "I-Thou" relationship—as is Gerard Manley Hopkins' term "inscape." Sadler labels this quality "a primary mode of attentiveness," while Marcel calls it more simply "presence." According to this description, there are no selfish, halfhearted, or disinterested players.

3. Spontaneity and Design

Play . . . creates an order out of imagination and therefore out of freedom.
—RUBEM ALVES[31]

The person who freely plays with loved ones (whether people or things) is prone to engage in very individual, spontaneous actions which might be thought foolish or risky in other contexts. There is a spontaneity and an abandon which characterizes such play. Any lover knows this. As we jump, skip, or swing through the air, as we tap our feet to the music or sing in the shower, our spirits soar. The viewer of art and the reader of a novel who surrender themselves to a new order of reality illustrate well both the validity of and the difficulties involved in such spontaneous freedom in the play experience. So does the father performing for his child, and the rugby player involved in a match. Though full of risk, such spontaneity opens a world of surprise. The father who makes comical faces to amuse his daughter may unintentionally cause her to cry, but he may also receive an unexpected hug. The rugby player is often injured, but the joy of a broken field-run cannot be duplicated. The reader of a novel must be open to the possibility that he or she will be a new person after reading the book, whether for good or for ill. So, too, the viewer of modern art.

Harvey Cox writes:

> The spirit of festivity [play], like a muse, has a mind of its own. It can fail to show up even when elaborate preparations have been made, leaving us all feeling a little silly. . . . Still, sometimes preparation for festivity does pay off. As Sister Corita says, "If you ice a cake, light sparklers and sing, something celebrative may happen."[32]

Spontaneity does not necessarily imply a lack of intention, as Cox's comment clearly suggests. The spontaneous freedom of a musical virtuoso comes as a result of and on the far side of hours of rigorous preparation. Similarly, the birthday party needs a cake baked beforehand. For the multiple experiences of play, there is no given sequence involved in turning from the larger world to a play world. The amount of planning or practice needed as the basis of play's spontaneity — or the lack of preparation — is totally dependent upon the complexity and form of the play world intended. The important thing is that at some point in all potentially playful experiences, the string between the player and his or her life-context must be cut. The structure of one's workaday world must be freely forsaken for another: that of the world of play.

Thus play's spontaneity is not to be confused with a lack of preparation or intention, nor should its vitality be equated with the merely chaotic.[33] For play is created by way of order, albeit an order which is freely embraced and which preserves the autonomy of the player. As Michael Novak points out in *The Joy of Sports,* "Observe toddlers at play, how they establish rules. 'This is water. This is land. You can't step on those. . . .' The spirit of play is the invention of rules. . . . The description of a fixed universe is the first and indispensable step of every free act."[34] The player is someone who chooses a set of rules, an order, as a vehicle for the free expression of his or her joy, power, and spontaneity. The rules are important not for their own sake but for the sake of the play activity itself. Take away play's design, refuse to play "according to Hoyle" (the eighteenth-century author whose explication of the rules of the game has become the standard for players), and play loses it significance. Without such rules, "it's not cricket."

Turning to specific instances of play, we find a form exhibited in every case. Michael Novak recognizes that "baseball, basketball, and football — like tennis, soccer, hockey, and countless other sports — are constituted as possibilities by bounded universes. Their liberties spring from fixed limits."[35] Anyone who has rushed the net in tennis to hit a successful shot, or stroked in a long putt, understands Novak's point. Having surrendered oneself to the rules and form of the game, one experiences, paradoxically, the full flush of freedom. A dance always has a form, as does a movie, a short story, a period of meditation, or a child's imaginary world. Jean Piaget observes that children as young as nine months old go through a ritualization process that begins when they playfully return to a fixed, but freely chosen, series of movements. In this regard children are similar to athletes, who also accept for the purposes of their play arbitrary and fanciful rules. (Why, for example, should there be hurdles to be jumped in a race?) Johan Huizinga's description of the musical experience can serve as a paradigm for all discussion of play's orderliness:

> Musical forms are in themselves play forms. Like play, music is based on the voluntary acceptance and strict application of a system of conventional rules—time, tone, melody, harmony, etc. . . . It is essentially a game, a contract valid within circumscribed limits, serving no useful purpose but yielding pleasure, relaxation, and an elevation of spirit.[36]

4. Non-Utilitarian, Yet Productive

Play is more than its definitions. It is where you realize the supreme importance and the utter insignificance of what you are doing.
—GEORGE SHEEHAN[37]

As we have observed, the player holds in tension a variety of polarities—a new world and the older one, a sense of both freedom and community, a spontaneity that has order. To this list we must add another attribute: a non-instrumentality which is nevertheless productive. Harvey Cox captures this facet of play well when he describes festivity as ". . . a brief recess from history making" which nonetheless restores our vision to re-create history.[38] "Phenomenologically, play is complete in itself," Richard Burke observes, "although it may serve other purposes as well."[39]

The fact that play must be pursued for its own sake, regardless of its consequences, provides a criterion by which to judge the activity of professional sports players. The professional athelete is a player according to our description only so long as he or she finds the nature of the sport complete and satisfying apart from the money and fame. If such outside consequences come along in the process, that is all right, but they must not be the motivation or focus of the play activity. Similarly, the children who play often develop coordination and learn to socialize in the process, but this is incidental to their playtime. "Play may serve all kinds of subsidiary, instrumental functions." Lee Gibbs observes,

> It has many biological, psychological, and cultural values. . . . Yet ultimately, like ritual, the purpose of play is in the play itself. If a person enters play only with useful, instrumental goals in mind, the activity ceases to be play. The most distinctive characteristic is that it is voluntary, spontaneous, a source of joy and amusement, an activity pursued exuberantly and fervently for its own sake.[40]

Unfortunately, many who are involved in sports have ceased to play. Lyman Bostrock, the former Minnesota baseball player who became a free agent and saw his salary rise from $20,000 to $450,000 a year, slumped so badly the next baseball season that he asked not to be paid his first month's salary. Wayne Garland, another disappointment as a highly paid free-agent, expressed the problem well: "I think what happened to me was that I was too anxious to prove to the fans I was worth the money." But it is not only money that can abort the play activity. Many factors can make a player take play too seriously. Fred van Dyke, for example, describes his fellow surfers as men who are usually out to prove something:

> Guys ride big waves for ego support, to compensate for something that is lacking in their lives. . . . Surfing should be fun. It's not fun. . . . Big-wave riders . . . have to go out there to prove they're not afraid, to prove their masculinity.[41]

Children know about play what adults often do not. (We might say children's play remains un-adult-erated.) Recreation specialists tell us that children resist adopting those games which have been composed or professionally remodeled for some "moral" purpose. Along similar lines, Stanford psychologists Mark Lepper and David Greene, in a paper entitled "Turning Play into Work," report on two groups of preschool children who were tested on their continuing interest in a certain play activity. One group was told that if they performed the activity, they would be rewarded by being allowed to play with their favorite toys. The other group was promised no reward. At the end of the activity both groups were allowed to play with the special toys. Interestingly, two weeks later, when tests were given to measure the ongoing interest in the original play activity, those children who had expected a reward showed significantly less interest in the activity. Because their play had become goal-oriented, they overlooked its pleasures. The activity had become purposive; it was work, not play.[42]

While the player is motivated by and focuses on the serious enjoyment of play's intrinsic value, he or she discovers, paradoxically, that play has external value. A person engages in play for its own sake, but it can have multiple benefits: (1) a continuing sense of delight or joy, (2) an affirmation of one's united self, (3) the creation of common bonds with one's world, (4) the emancipation of one's spirit so that it moves outward toward the sacred, and (5) the relativization of one's workaday world.

Writing about the joy of sports, Michael Novak recalls the pleasure of following the exploits of George Blanda, a forty-three-year-old football player who passed and kicked his team, the Oakland Raiders, to victory week after week in 1970. His accomplishments were almost magical: "He touched something vulnerable in the breasts of millions . . . for those who saw the actual deeds, their beauty spoke for themselves; their excellence pleased; something true shone out. The tales of *Gawain and the Green Knight, The Song of Roland, The Exploits of Ivanhoe* — these are the ancient games in which human beings have for centuries found refreshment."[43] Basketball great Bill Bradley describes his joy in sports in this way:

> What I'm addicted to are nights when something special happens on the court. . . . It is far more than a passing emotion. It is as if a lightning bolt strikes, bringing insight into an uncharted area of human experience. . . . It goes beyond the competition that brings goose pimples or the ecstasy of victory. . . . A back-door play that comes with perfect execution at a critical time charges the crowd but I sense an immediate transporting enthusiasm and a feeling that everything is in perfect balance.[44]

The delight experienced during play and remembered afterward is not limited to athletics. It is felt by the musician, the theater-goer, and the dancer. Moreover, this joy is not an isolated emotion, as Bradley's comment suggests. It is itself related to at least three other feelings arising during the playtime — a sense of personal unity and wholeness, a gratefulness for the "common world" of the play community, and a recognition of life's fundamental sacredness.

In his book *Religion and Leisure in America,* Robert Lee states: "Leisure is the growing time of the human spirit. Leisure provides the occasion for learning and freedom, for growth and expression, for rest and restoration, for rediscovering life in its entirety."[45] In this statement Lee recognizes a second consequence of play, although he comes close to overburdening play in the process. As Jurgen Moltmann warns, "Don't turn play into a total ideology. Don't be a kill-joy (*Spielverderber*)."[46] Lee's point is that play does quicken our sense of possibility and stimulate our imagination, making us in the process more fully human. A second consequence of play is that players become totally involved physically, emotionally, and mentally; they play only in the wholeness of their being. George Sheehan writes about experiencing this sense of involvement when he runs:

> There are times . . . I come home from running a race in Central Park, when I don't know who won or where I finished or what time I ran. My family wonders then why I went. Why I spent the day coming and going and endured that cruel hour on those rolling hills. I have no logical answer. I simply know that for that hour I was whole and true and living at the top of my powers. That hour was life intensified.[47]

Sheehan is not the only one who describes running in these terms. Runners often speak of breaking through a "wall" of pain and experiencing a commingling of body and spirit, an intimate ecstasy in which one senses a fundamental harmony in life.

A third quality of play is its capacity to create strong bonds between people. The intersubjectivity—the "interplay," or communion, so common in play—serves to re-create for the participant a sense of his or her common world. Johan Huizinga draws upon this fact, as he finds the element of play basic to all cultures. He believes culture must be viewed *sub specie ludi,* for, he says, "Law and order, commerce and profit, craft and art, poetry, wisdom and science, all are rooted in the primaeval soil of play." By this Huizinga does not mean to equate culture and play but only to suggest that "in its earliest phases culture has the play-character, that it proceeds in the shape and mold of play."[48] Although Huizinga is a bit extravagant, his general direction is unquestionably correct. As Gabriel Vahanian states:

"Indeed, authentic leisure can only remind us of the task of being human. It can only help us re-member our humanity."[49] In the comic strip *Peanuts*, Snoopy recognizes this fact. In one cartoon he is first pictured dancing alone and exclaiming, "To live is to dance!" But after he joins Lucy and dances with her, he concludes, "To dance is to live!"[50]

Walter Kerr alludes to a fourth possible consequence of one's play activity when he writes of the awareness that can result from play:

> It is a knowledge that breeds affection, what Conrad called "the latent feeling of fellowship with all creation." It renews our pleasure in the universe. More than that. As our being touches other being, and lets it flow into us, we are mysteriously aware that our own being has been increased. . . . Something like re-creation runs in us like a tide.[51]

A similar sentiment is expressed by Roger Bannister, the first runner to break the record for the four-minute mile. He tells of running along the beach as a boy and being overcome by sheer joy:

> I was startled, and frightened, by the tremendous excitement that so few steps could create. . . . The earth seemed almost to move with me. . . . No longer conscious of my movement, I discovered a new unity with nature. I had found a new source of power and beauty, a source I never dreamt existed.[52]

While Kerr and Bannister do not speak explicitly in religious terms, others have forthrightly labeled such "mysterious" experiences "sacred" in character. Thus Harvey Cox believes that play provides an opening to a region that is real but hard "to discern and whose name is less definite," that region beyond the horizon of consciousness we call history. According to Cox, there is a sense of awe, intuition, and ecstasy that opens up the player to what Mircea Eliade calls "cosmos" and Teilhard de Chardin has named the "divine milieu."[53]

Gerardus Van der Leeuw expresses a similar conviction when he writes about drama. He believes that drama is sometimes capable of expressing the holy. "Here we can find a religious aspect," he says. "A man who reaches the background of life, its ultimate basis, comes upon a boundary. Broadening and deepening, the sudden experiences of life as a unity bring with them the suspicion of holiness." About dance, Van der Leeuw says, "The dance is the discovery of movement external to man, but which first gives him his true, actual movement. In the dance shines the recognition of God, himself, moving and thereby moving the world." About music, Van der Leeuw suggests, "The inclination to the absolute, which is called silence," is the sacred extremity of music.[54] What Van der Leeuw describes has been expressed in a more down-to-earth way on a poster: "The 'consecrated spot' cannot be distinguished from the playground."[55] And vice versa. We are also reminded of Johan Huizinga's belief that in play "man's consciousness that he is embedded in a sacred order of things finds its first, highest and holiest expression."[56]

It is not only students of culture like Van der Leeuw and Huizinga who have found in play a possible sacred dimension. Theologians have also commented upon this. Harvey Cox is one; Karl Barth is another. In discussing Mozart's genius, Barth says he thinks Mozart's music has a religious dimension — "a childlike knowledge of the center of all things — including the knowledge of their beginning and their end."[57] Karl Rahner links the playful with the transcendent in a similar way. He states: "For the greater his [the player's] freedom [mental and physical] with regard to the objective world, the stronger can and should be his transcendental experience of his dependence on the absoluteness of God."[58]

And lest one imagine a hypothetical hierarchy in play in which the arts retain this ability to mediate the presence of the divine while such "lower" forms of play as athletics remain puerile, let me again quote Michael Novak:

> I love it when the other side is winning and there are only moments left; I love it when it would be reasonable to be reconciled to defeat, but one will not, cannot; I love it when a last set of calculated, reckless, free, and impassioned efforts is crowned with success. When I see others play that way, I am full of admiration, of gratitude. That is the way I believe the human race should live. When human beings actually accomplish it, it is for me as if the intentions of the Creator were suddenly limpid before our eyes: as though into the fiery heart of the Creator we had momentary insight.[59]

This is the recognition that Harry Angstrom has in Updike's novel *Rabbit, Run,* after he lofts a perfect golf shot.[60] This, too, is a moment of Grace—a childlike knowledge of the center of all things.

Participants in play can be opened outward in two directions. Through their play experience they can be granted a vision both of the re-creation of "man" (individually and communally) and of that sacred ground in which humankind is rooted. According to Gerardus Van der Leeuw, "The game points beyond itself: downward, to the simple, ordinary rhythm of life; upward, to the highest forms of existence."[61] Unfortunately, such a transcendent awareness is absent from much of contemporary life in America. The absolute claims of our technological age and the imperialistic pressure of our work have conspired to produce what someone has called "the tyranny of the immediate." Our world has taken on a reduced size. Nevertheless, play is one way out of this dilemma, a possible first step in the contemporary person's pilgrimage from bondage to freedom. But play serves this purpose only incidentally and *ex post facto,* presenting by its very existence the possibility of a different social order. Play "provides an alternative," suggests Cox, "to either cowed submission or empty nihilism."[62] Players know themselves to be more real than the system; their captivity is less real than their play world. Such relativization of one's workaday world is a fifth and final consequence of the play experience.

If a person is not able to play, he is easily bewitched or possessed by his own seriousness or the seriousness of another. Inhumanity is the result. Play breaks through such barriers and thus serves as a prologue to and/or a check upon a life of freedom. Rubem Alves, a third-world theologian, clearly sees this as a consequence of play. Responding to criticism that play is "kid's business," he argues instead for the prophetic and political meaning of play.[63] He believes that our society has become oppressive and repressive, and that we need to let go of many of the rules imposed upon our lives. The time for creative imagination has arrived. Magic, play, and utopian dreams are the foundation for his future community of faith.[64]

By way of summary, then, I am suggesting that play is important for the continued well-being of people, individually and collectively. Play relativizes our "over-seriousness" toward life, filling us with a spirit of joy and delight that carries over into all aspects of our existence. This attitude is based in and fosters the tacit recognition of a restored humanity that senses its rootedness in life's fundamental sacredness. Play has, in short, an external value that reaches far beyond the boundary of the play world. But this is the case only when the player "forgets" play's consequences and focuses solely upon the intrinsic value of the play. The authentic player knows that play's value is contained by the playtime and the playground. As John Cage writes:

> A purposeful purposelessness
>   and purposeless play.
> This play, however, is an
>   affirmation of life.
> Not an attempt to bring order out of chaos,
>   not to suggest improvements in creation,
>   but simply a way of waking up
> the very life we are living.[65]

The Boundaries of Play

It is a sin to eat inferior ice cream.

—ERIC GILL[66]

In his preface to Hugo Rahner's *Man at Play,* Walter Ong makes an observation typical of commentators on play: "The world of play is the world of freedom itself—of activity for its own sake, of spontaneity, of pure realization." Ong is atypical, however, in his pointing out that work, too, "is an expression of freedom and joy" when authentically pursued.[67] Ong rightly understands that it is false to draw a distinction between play as individual, free, and spontaneous, and work as collective, intentional, and ordered. Both the worker and the player bring to their worlds the social and the private, the ordered and the spontaneous, the free participation and the destined response. This understanding of the general human shape of play provides us with a final criterion with which to delimit play's boundaries.

Unlike many who currently write on the subject, I want in light of the above discussion to distinguish the play of humans from the "play" of animals. Recreationalist Charles Brightbill is too inclusive in describing play as "the free, pleasurable, immediate, and natural expression of animals."[68] So, too, is Walter Kerr, who believes that animals first discovered play and left it to man as a legacy.[69] What I have been arguing is that the activity I have described as play requires an atittude uniquely human. The cat playing with a rubber ball *seems* to be playing, but its consciousness is different from that of the human player. Further exploration of the attitudes of animals is necessary here, and the lines of demarcation blur, but the "play" of animals seems best understood as instinctive, almost automatic movement rather than play. Play, I am suggesting, belongs not merely to the phenomenal world but to the intelligent world. It is not "a general organic activity, but a specifically human one," as Ernst Cassirer argues.[70]

Play's attitudinal locus helps define not only the border between animal and human "play," but also a second boundary— that between authentic and inauthentic play. Play is neither escapism nor melancholic resignation. It is neither obsessive nor merely empty, mechanical ritual. Much of what is commonly labeled "play" fits into these categories, however, and must be understood as not being play at all. In his book *In Praise of Play,* Robert Neale discusses in detail these perversions of play: when peace is "inaction"; when freedom is bondage to one need in our psyche which is dominant; when delight is turned into a work agenda; when illusion is maintained at the expense of other needs and is a form of mental illness; when the story is believed, the time limits ignored, and pretending becomes pretension; when a game is played at the expense of others, breaking the rules; when the risk of adventure is perverted and the gamble removed or fatalistically accepted; or when play is done in secret. In these cases the "player" is not really playing at all.[71] Most gambling and most magic can thus be viewed as inauthentic play—play that is deficient because of the attitude of the player. When Walter Kerr quotes Eric Gill, he offers a less obvious example. Gill believed that it was a sin to eat inferior ice cream. "Mr. Gill was right," suggests Kerr, "and his rightness has nothing to do with calories or ordinary human perversity. . . . To eat ice cream that displeases is to engage in an act which denies its own nature. . . ."[72]

Johan Huizinga is similarly concerned with recognizing the bastardization of play. Much "which to a superficial eye [has] all the appearance of play and might be taken for permanent play-tendencies . . . [is], in point of fact, nothing of the sort." He calls such inauthentic play "puerilism," the blend of adolescence and barbarity. Trivial recreation, crude sensationalism, gregariousness, intolerant sectarian clubs — these are all examples of puerilism, according to Huizinga. Writing during the Nazi build-up to World War II, Huizinga concluded: "According to our definition of play, puerilism is to be distinguished from playfulness. . . . The spectacle of a society rapidly goose-stepping into helotry is, for some, the dawn of the millennium. We believe them to be in error."[73] Here, surely, is Huizinga's hidden agenda for writing *Homo Ludens*. Given his contemporary world, in which the elements of play were being perverted and misused for totalitarian ends, he called his contemporaries back to an awareness of play authentically conceived. Without a conscious disruption of ongoing events and a recognition of the inutility of play, without a combination of order and spontaneity, freedom and love, what seems on the surface to be play is merely a false semblance of it.

The 1972 Munich Olympics provide us a model by which to observe the differentiation between authentic and inauthentic play. The Olympics were meant to be a paradigm of play activity. For these Games, a playtime was set aside and a special playing field was built. In theory they were organized as a parenthesis in life, devoid of political consideration.[74] For this reason, when the Arab terrorists struck within the Olympic Village, the playing field was not immediately open to the German military. Although the compound was on German soil, it was thought of as a world community for those two weeks. Within the Games there was a strict adherence to the rules. Thus Rich Demont, who won the 400-meter freestyle swim race, was disqualified when it was discovered that he had traces of a drug used for asthma in his system. Because drugs can give a player outside control, can allow the player to manipulate the play experience, drug use — even use not intended to improve performance — is illegal. In the 1972 Games there was a sense of risk and adventure; most lost in their events, in fact. But in another sense all those who played succeeded. The joy and excitement generated by the experience, the sense of commonality with fellow players from around the world, the opportunity to participate freely with one's entire being — this gave all the players a new outlook on their everyday world. Or so the script read in advance.

In reality, the terrorism in Munich infringed upon the Olympic play world and prematurely ended the Games. True, the Games continued on, obscenely, in form, but they were no longer a parenthesis in life. In the face of the ultimate—death—play ceased to be. Thus, what people remember about the 1972 Games is not the joyful community but the horror of the massacre of the Israeli team. Moreover, regardless of the killings, much of what should have been play was not. The Olympics became a political arena. African athletes threatened a boycott. East German athletes were only the most extreme examples among many who were at the Games because a series of tests and special treatment had pointed them joylessly toward it. Duane Bobick, the American boxer, seemed intent only on impressing the world so that his professional contract would be more lucrative. The morality of politics (or the lack of it) and the reality of the workaday world intruded into the play world of the Munich Olympics. Unfortunately, the spirit of play was lost in the shuffle.[75]

Dietrich Bonhoeffer, writing from prison shortly before his death, addressed his godson, Dietrich Bethge, on the occasion of the infant's baptism, which he could not witness: "Music, as your parents understand and practice it, will help to dissolve your perplexities and purify your character and sensibility, and in times of care and sorrow will keep a ground-base of joy alive in you."[76] Bonhoeffer's advice is analogous to the conclusions in this chapter. In these times of stress—in a society pressured on all sides, moving toward its breaking point—play can purify our sensibility, make us open again to the gifts of God's goodness which surround us. Furthermore, play can open us up to understand life's rhythms and limits, dissolving some of the perplexity of things—even death itself. Finally, play can keep that gracious "ground-base of joy" alive in all of us, and so prepare us for, and help sustain us within, our ongoing life of faith.

III

Play:
Three Theological Options

Our dream pictures of the Happy Place where suf-
fering and evil are unknown are of two kinds, the
Edens and the New Jerusalems. Though it is pos-
sible for the same individual to imagine both, it
is unlikely that his interest in both will be equal
and I suspect that between the Arcadian whose
favorite daydream is of Eden, and the Utopian
whose favorite daydream is of New Jerusalem there
is a characterological gulf.

—W. H. AUDEN[1]

MANY CHRISTIAN THEOLOGIANS CAN BE CHARACTER-
ized as belonging to one of two camps. There are, on the right,
those theologians clustering around the individualistic orienta-
tions of a Paul Tillich or a Rudolph Bultmann, and on the left,
those moving outward from the more socially dominated schemes
of a Karl Barth or a Dietrich Bonhoeffer. The disciples of the
former have been concerned with emphasizing the need for a
radical redefinition of personal faith, while those finding their
roots in the latter have often focused on the need to radically
restructure society and the Church. The one group has moved
inward from an aesthetic conviction, having a vision of Eden;
the other has moved outward from an ethic, having a vision of
the New Jerusalem. One group has understood the Kingdom of
God in Arcadian terms, the other in Utopian terms.

Such a comparison is, of course, both overstated and incomplete. Nevertheless, it allows us to discern the general split
in much of academic theology today. Both sides begin with a
problem concerning the present, but each poses a different question. The one asks, How can I celebrate life? The other asks,
How can we change the world? In seeking answers, the one has

concerned itself with individual healing, the other with political liberation.

What is surprising in the context of this book is the desire of both "life-liberators" and "world-changers" to explore the phenomenon of play as a possible means toward their respective visions of wholeness. For those on both sides, however, play has proven a continuing problem, for it has remained within work-dominated categories. Christian theologians have scarcely fared better than general society in understanding the nature and importance of play. In terms of our discussion in Chapter One, the theological left has attempted to include play within its work agenda of political liberation—within, that is, its updated work ethic. The theological right, on the other hand, reacting against such extrinsic goals, has adopted a new set of rules, turning its competitive impulse inward. Play has assumed a central place in this altered agenda, too, self-expression and fulfillment becoming the goal. Whether "play as politics" or "play as total ideology," the result has been the same: play has been reduced to something less than itself.

Before moving our discussion appreciably forward, it will prove instructive to consider at some length the ideas of representative theologians from both of these camps who have written on play. Their struggles to articulate play's rightful place in the Christian life will focus the issue for us theologically as well as prepare us to explore other possible theological venues. Sam Keen and Jurgen Moltmann are two such writers. Keen, a theological post-Tillichian with philosophical roots in Marcel and Heidegger, has been almost preoccupied with the phenomenon of play as a means of personal healing. His books and articles, such as *Apology for Wonder,* "Manifesto for a Dionysian Theology," *To a Dancing God,* and *Telling Your Story,* all center on the experience of play.[2] Jurgen Moltmann, a theological post-Barthian with philosophical roots in Bloch and Hegel, has explored play much less frequently. But he, too, has found in play a means of enfleshing his theology of hope and liberation. In his article " 'How Can I Play, When I'm in a Strange Land?' " and his subsequent essay "The First Liberated Men in Creation," which was an expansion of his previous reflection and which was published in English as *Theology of Play,* we find his most direct writings on the topic.[3]

But neither man will provide contemporary Christians with the most helpful clarifications of play. At best, they are useful foils. Instead, theological insight comes from somewhat surprising quarters, from the "non-theological" pens of Peter Berger and C. S. Lewis. Both men, from their differing perspectives on culture—Berger as a sociologist of religion and Lewis as a professor of English literature—have allowed play to be the activity we have described in Chapter Two. Moreover, each has addressed himself specifically to play's "religious" impulse—its potential for opening us up to the sacred dimensions of reality. Perhaps their primarily academic moorings in the world of culture have made these lay-theologians particularly sensitive to the nature and implications of play. Whatever the reason, Lewis's *Surprised by Joy* and Berger's *A Rumor of Angels* show real discernment. Thus in this chapter we will begin with the writings of Keen and Moltmann and conclude with the thoughts of Berger and, more particularly, of C. S. Lewis.

Play as Total Ideology: Sam Keen

Sam Keen is a former Associate Professor of Philosophy and Christian Faith at Louisville Presbyterian Theological Seminary and more recently Director of the Esalen Institute Theological Residence Program and a contributing editor of *Psychology Today*. He has moved increasingly from theology toward psychology and from working within an institutional structure to one much more individualistic and free-lance. Throughout this varied professional career, Keen has focused on finding personal answers to life's meaning. Taking his clues from Gabriel Marcel and Paul Tillich, Keen has understood the theologian's task to be that of describing a means of healing for humankind's "disease," its estrangement. Thus his *theology* has been functionally synonymous with his *therapy*. This is the key to understanding Keen, for when one realizes that he thinks that theology and psychology are functionally equivalent, there emerges a general shape and common direction to his otherwise many-faceted endeavors.

In his writings, which are strongly autobiographical (and thus oriented to the white, upper-middle-class male), Keen first asks how we overcome the "dis-ease" of humankind. He then envisions a new person and prescribes a cure that will produce the desired results. What Keen offers is a new theological anthropology, a new therapeutics. He states: "Every form of therapy, whether it is carried on in churches, growth centers, consulting rooms or wisdom schools rests upon a vision of what man might become, a diagnosis of his present unhappiness and a prescription for how he may move toward fulfillment."[4]

A. The Diagnosis

Keen thinks today's Americans are ill at ease with themselves, and thus are less than fully human. The sources of this discomfort are multiple, but the chief one is that people in the West live under a Promethean illusion, attempting to evade the reality of their vulnerability and transience. Keen labels such "dis-eased" persons *Homo Faber* (man the fabricator, or worker) — man bent on creating his own meaning by eliminating all elements of mystery. Obsessed with the need for clarity, *Homo Faber* has what might be labeled "the scrubbing compulsion of the mind."[5] His self-image, according to Keen, "is so exclusively 'masculine' that it makes impossible an appreciation of the dignity of the more 'feminine' modes of perceiving and relating to the world; it majors in molding and manipulation and neglects accepting and welcoming."[6] Sterile both in environment and attitude, *Homo Faber* finds it impossible to participate sensually in a way that will create authentic life.

For Keen, the dis-eased person as *Homo Faber* is the individual who has destroyed both human wholeness and the possibility for new life by denying the "feminine" in favor of the "masculine." Keen offers an alternate yet similar appraisal of our contemporary "dis-ease" when he speaks of the destructive bifurcation of individuals into bodies and minds. Rather than accept our bodily humanity with its limits (chief of which is death), we have sought to live with the illusion that our bodies are mere objects to be used or abused. We have constructed a body "to work, not to play. . . . It's a capitalistic body — a body ruled by the head."[7] We in the West have become too cerebral, too gnostic, Christian theology being a chief supporter of this heresy. Keen tells us that he himself once suffered from this illness. He describes himself in his mid-thirties as having had a "good, stylish, serious, productive, disciplined, neurotic, death-defying American body."[8]

Keen is suggesting that Western society's present "dis-ease" is attitudinal. It may be described as our prejudice favoring the masculine over the feminine, or our preoccupation with the mind over the body. It may also be categorized as a penchant for the Apollonian over the Dionysian. The modern individual has too often subjugated the spontaneous to the orderly, the possible to the necessary, the enthusiastic to the reasonable, the wonderful to the regular.[9] In yet another description, Keen identifies our current "dis-ease" as our inability to view life as a "story," to integrate past, present, and future into a meaningful whole.[10] The metaphysical myths of our tradition no longer confer identity upon us today. We have lost our unity of life; past, present, and future find no common ground. Lacking a story, we must form our identity in a void.

In his book *Telling Your Story*, Keen summarizes these various descriptions of our contemporary distress:

> The dis-ease of modern man's psyche is more of a vacuum than a thorn in the flesh. We are alienated, disgraced, frustrated, and bored because of what hasn't happened, because of potentialities we have not explored. Few of us *know* the fantastic characters, emotions, perceptions and demons that inhabit the theaters that are our minds.[11]

"Man" does not *know* that within him resides the "feminine" as well as the "masculine," the body as well as the mind, the Dionysian as well as the Apollonian, the present as well as the past and the future. Keen's therapeutic psychology, his theological anthropology, is thus committed to helping an individual shed his limited identity as a "dis-eased" person in order that he might *know* his full and balanced humanity.

B. The Vision

According to Keen, life fully in accord with human nature is "graceful, light, and playful."[12] It is based in wonder, hope, and trust. Keen's new individual is similar to that proposed by the counter-therapies in psychology. He is "sensuous, immediate, playful"—one "whose prime vocation will be enjoyment, not labor, and whose best work will be very much like play."[13] In his writings Keen has attempted to portray the new person he envisions in a variety of ways. But chief among these has been the new person as *Homo Tempestivus* and as "graceful man."

Homo Tempestivus is literally "timely man."[14] He is sometimes Dionysian, at other times Apollonian, depending on what is most appropriate to the occasion. Within this model, health is judged in terms of balance, for the human spirit demands both wilderness and home, wonder and welcome, adventure and security, the Dionysian and the Apollonian. As Keen says, "A philosophical definition of health, creative life, or authentic selfhood must incorporate the dominant emphases of these two modes of being in the world and their respective models of man. . . . Health is to be found in balance, in wholeness—in polychrome existence."

One need not choose between wonder and action, grace and responsibility, for the "healthy personality is structured upon a principle of oscillation."[15]

Taking his cue from Ecclesiastes, Keen believes everything is beautiful in its own time. The problem with this scheme is that Keen both misreads the biblical wisdom tradition and seems to equate work with the Apollonian and play with the Dionysian. We will return to these difficulties in due course. For now it is sufficient to observe that Keen understands the healthy or mature person to be one who moves gracefully between the Dionysian and Apollonian modes of being in the world according to the changing seasons and crises of life. *Homo Tempestivus* always seeks to act appropriately. Keen suggests that the best metaphor to illuminate this style is that of the dance: "The wise man is a dancer; he hears the music issuing from his situation. He is sensitive to his partners, and moves boldly to commit himself to the rhythmic patterns that emerge. . . . The sense of timing which is the essence of wisdom comes only when one trusts oneself to the dance."[16]

Keen believes that *Homo Tempestivus*—the fully mature individual—"like an athlete or a dancer . . . moves among the ambiguities and limitations of existence with a *gracefulness* that appears to the spectator effortless and spontaneous."[17] Such a "graceful man," whether viewed athletically, socially, or theologically, is one who has "*trust* in the context within which action must take place and *confidence* in the ability of the self to undertake appropriate action."[18] As Keen continues his description of a graceful individual in *To a Dancing God,* notions of integration supersede those of oscillation. The "graceful man" is now portrayed as the mature person who is willing to be his *whole* self in a state of relaxed freedom, to dwell creatively in the *holiness* of his own native soil, to be "at home" in the moving resonance of the present. For Keen, grace is having the courage to be satisfied. The "graceful man" is the one who has been inhabited by the "dancing god," that is, life itself; he is the person whose style is serendipitous who finds grace in the most modest and hidden places. The graceful individual freely integrates not only the Apollonian and the Dionysian but the present, past, and future into a meaningful whole. The best metaphor to describe this individual is, again, the dancer. Zorba is Keen's graceful person par excellence: one who dances "with the whole spirit."[19]

C. The Prescription

Keen's prescription for healing "dis-ease" and returning individuals to their intended wholeness can be summarized in one word: play. Whether by accepting gracefully the "wonder-ful" in life, or by integrating past, present, and future within one's personal story, or by giving oneself over to the visceral and erotic, Keen proposes that we turn from the acid soil of a Promethean view of life and embrace instead an attitude of wonder.[20] We must lose our illusions (in Keen's words, we must become "dis-illusioned") about self-mastery and accept life as a given. Only then are "we set free to admire rather than possess, to enjoy rather than exploit, to accept rather than grasp."[21] A wondering individual is able to find the graceful in the ordinary—in a cup of tea or the caress of the winds. He dwells within the logic of the "player," freely accepting the limits (of life's game) as gifts.[22] Recognizing his boundaries, he is able to turn to a mode of perceiving and celebrating that is spontaneous, immediate, and erotic. Such a "wonder-ful" person has the capacity for "sustained and continued delight, marvel, amazement, and enjoyment."[23] He is truly a perpetual "player."

If one's dis-ease is in part an existence without a meaningful story by which to integrate present, past, and future, then a prescription for wholeness will also include a means by which to write anew one's story. Only then can one be "wonder-ful." According to Keen, the ground of theology, or storytelling, is no longer outside the human community, God being "dead"; thus Keen feels we must shift our focus to the individual and the commonplace.[24] In order to overcome my dis-ease, my dis-grace, Keen suggests that "I can proceed by telling my story."[25] Such playful autobiography is, at its core, a confession of faith. It professes belief that there is in the native ground of one's own experience, one's history, that which testifies to the holy and thereby unites all humankind.

According to Keen, our gracefulness, our ability to be "wonder-ful," requires that we become fully incarnate in our own bodies and historical situations. To tell one's story is to incarnate one's history. To be erotic is to come home to one's body. "Incarnation, if it is anything more than a 'once-upon-a-time' story," suggests Keen, "means grace is carnal, healing comes through the flesh."[26] The inner harmony resulting from affirming one's story needs to be matched by an outer harmony resulting from an affirmation of one's body. To be erotic and to tell your story are two sides of the same coin. "Trust your body," says Keen. "Do what feels good."[27] For as a person is in his body, so he will be in the world. Thus Keen urges as a prescription for the "dis-eased" individual that his "real, literal, carnal body" be "resensitized and educated in the sacredness which lies hidden in its feelings."[28]

Whether advocating giving oneself over to the ecstatic and wonderful, or telling one's story, or doing what feels good as "body-minds," Keen's prescriptive therapy is broadly centered in the experience of play. How are we to *know* ourselves fully and thus escape our present dis-ease? Keen would suggest that play is the medicine which will restore health. In the experience of play, whether it is reflecting on one's story, hiking in the mountains, or making love, we have the opportunity to experience ourselves vibrantly and authentically—to know our real selves to be other than our present states of "dis-ease."

Is This Theology?

What is there in Keen's analysis which makes his play-therapy theology—particularly given his acceptance of the death of

God (i.e., his rejection of the Christian story as rendering life ultimately meaningful)? Keen has answered just such a question by suggesting that his concern is a phenomenological one, centering on those places where the holy is most manifest. Where have you been both trembling and fascinated? Keen asks. Keen says that when he is asked such a question, he almost inevitably responds in one of three ways: (1) " 'Well, I was on a mountaintop'; or 'I was by the ocean' " — i.e., the experiences of nature are often still sacred to the modern individual; (2) "When we had twenty thousand people in Louisville, Kentucky, with Martin Luther King and we sang. . . . 'We Shall Overcome' . . . we trembled" — i.e., being truly "in community" can be sacred; and (3) "sexuality is a place of trembling, both of the fear and of the promise" — i.e., sexuality is still a place where the holy resides.[29]

By means of such examples, Keen relates the notion of play to that of the sacred, consciously returning to the thesis of Rudolf Otto's *The Idea of the Holy.* In this book Otto distinguishes several earmarks of that which is holy or sacred. There is, he says, a *mysterium* due to the presence of the Other which has two defining characteristics: it is simultaneously *tremendum* (awesome) and *fascinans* (desirable).[30] And where is that mystery experienced primarily today? In our play, asserts Keen. "Whatever functions to unify life, to assure its meaningfulness, to provide what Tillich called an 'ultimate concern,' " Keen writes, "is experienced as *mysterium: tremendum et fascinans.*"[31]

Religion traditionally functioned to nourish and restore one's sense of basic trust. In our modern age, however, not all will find an overtly religious, transcendental form of trust compatible with their epistemological foundations. Keen thinks some people will want to remain religious agnostics, locating the sacred in "flesh, things, and event or not at all." Holiness will be "homogenized into the quotidian." But this need not cause us to despair. Even for these people, their ability to wonder, to accept life's mystery gracefully and gratefully, will allow them also "to credit the context that nourishes and creates [them] as being worthy of trust." For Keen, whether we talk about this context as "God" is not so important as whether we retain that sense of wonder which keeps us aware that ours is a holy place.[32]

Such is Sam Keen's theology "at a minimum."[33] Keen asks,

"What is there worth preserving in the Christian tradition?" and his phenomenological answer is found on the level of anthropology, particularly in the person as player. In play we can experience the numinous; our sense of basic trust in life can be nourished and restored. Keen's theology remains *"humble,"* *"agnostic"* —discovering the sacred on native soil through a "reawakening of the *body*" and a reaffirmation of one's personal *story.* Keen's theology centers on common, natural grace, which he finds rooted within the human experience. With theology through the ages, his theology-therapy seeks the healing of persons but locates the source of that healing not in the distant but the proximate, not in the supernatural but the natural.

An Evaluation

Much can be learned from Keen's theology-therapy. His assessment of contemporary society's ills extends the lines of our argument in Chapter One. The work-dominated models of Western society have been destructive of authentic personhood. The "masculine" has predominated, as has the cerebral and the Apollonian. We need to abandon our Promethean quest and accept life gracefully. Moreover, the sacred does need to be rediscovered in the common events of life—"in a cup of tea and the caress of the winds." As both an iconoclast and a spokesman for the value of play in human experience, Keen needs to be heard. Nevertheless, his writing is seriously deficient.

This is so because central to Keen's thought has been his belief that all theology, including a theological understanding of play, must be defined solely in terms of one's own autobiography ("I may speak of grace only in the first person").[34] This solipsistic reduction of religious authority to personal experience has led Keen to characterize incorrectly both theology and the play experience itself.

Theologically, Keen has been seduced into caricaturing Christian experience according to his reaction to his Fundamentalist upbringing. In his eyes, his experience as a youth within the church was sterile, wooden, legalistic, repressive—in short, lacking in grace. His more general understanding of Christian experience has been colored by this personal frustration, with the result that he has reduced the Christian life to the mere memory of a past event (he labels this "Israel") which seeks to make its believers hard, tight, and controlled. Keen believes that Christianity stresses the supernatural rather than the natural, the extraordinary rather than the ordinary, the transcendent rather than the subterranean, the past rather than the present, law rather than grace, spirit rather than body, substance rather than symbol. For Keen, the result is that Christianity has little if anything to do with play and must therefore be rejected.[35]

Keen's commitment to theological autobiography has led him not only to caricature Christianity but also to romanticize his resultant agnosticism. Although, according to Keen, we cannot claim any sure knowledge of God, theology can nevertheless use the word *God* to serve an indispensable function.[36] We need to remain hopeful if we are to maintain our sanity, Keen asserts.[37] Thus the idea of God can function to unify our needful affirmations about this unknown source — affirmations of "the trustworthiness of the mystery which surrounds [our] existence." As to how such an assertion is possible (even if it is advantageous), Keen tentatively suggests that if our dominant conviction is that our bodies and feelings can be trusted, "the likelihood is that" we will adopt a liberal view of ultimate reality.[38] Keen's personal history as an affluent Anglo-Saxon male seems to become crucial at this point, for it allows him an optimism that is incredible considering the tooth-and-nail progression of world history.

As for his notion of play, despite his occasional attempts to make play sensitive to the communal and the disciplined, Keen has wrongly equated play with one of life's poles — the Dionysian. For Keen, play is "a touch of madness." If play does not lack rules altogether, the rules can at least be changed at will by the player. The person at play knows no limits; he is ecstatic and wonderful — embracing the individual and dynamic while fleeing from the sanctions imposed both by other players and by rules. Again, Keen's personal history seems determinative in this skewing of play's nature. During the first part of his adult life, Keen was a workaholic, and felt stifled and bored. Thus he has attempted to throw off life's past chains by fleeing from work into play. If work was wrongly characterized by the Apollonian, play now becomes exclusively the Dionysian. Keen admits there are times in life for the orderly, the rational, and the communal, but such activity is not play. Human life is seen as an oscillation between the irrational and rational, the Dionysian and Apollonian, play and non-play.

Moreover, because of his personal history, Keen has largely ignored matters of social ethics in his discussion of play, despite his desire to become *Homo Tempestivus,* that timely man who responds appropriately to life around him. To give but one example, in his book *Telling Your Story,* Keen states:

> That society is unjust often means that one man's gift is another man's wound. Scarsdale and Harlem, wealth and poverty, privilege and oppression co-exist in unholy symbiosis. But things are more than what they seem. Rich is better than hungry, but injustice may create a supportive community among victims while exploiters suffer anomie. Anxiety and madness can be the price of creative genius. Gifts and wounds fit together like yang and yin.[39]

Such egocentric and, I suspect, ultimately cynical beliefs run roughshod over the ethical. It is easy and correct to say that a playful life in Scarsdale (Keen's life) has its problems. But it is obscene for the person in Scarsdale to suggest that his pain is somehow on a par with, or can be balanced off against, that of the person in Harlem. Keen proposes naively that somehow his privileged play in ignorance and unconscious support of others' oppressed conditions is the best means toward realizing authentic humanness for all. But clearly, the oppressor does not help the oppressed merely by freeing himself through play; he must also work to change structures and to overcome the results of his former and continuing oppressiveness. Keen seems to find little if any meaning in "man-as-maker" or "man-for-others" (to say nothing of woman). He would have us believe that an individual can become free only by first playing in his own garden. One suspects, however, that such rhetoric can be reduced to "eat, drink, and be merry, for tomorrow we die."

Play as Politics: Jurgen Moltmann

Like Sam Keen, Jurgen Moltmann seeks the liberation of humankind from its modern afflictions, and so gives a functional cast to his theology; he too offers a *diagnosis* of the world's misery, a *vision* of the world's possibilities, and a *prescription* for liberation, i.e., salvation. But similarities between these two men stop here. For while Keen begins consistently with the phenomenon of play (wonder), he moves only cautiously and in conclusion to the overtly theological ("theology is phenomenology"). Moltmann takes the opposite approach, interpreting play in light of an already carefully developed theological system. His theological direction can be summarized in one word: hope. Moltmann offers a far-ranging biblical dogmatic centering on the concept of promise.

According to Moltmann, Christian theology presupposes a "natural" element with which the "supernatural" character of its own vision can be contrasted. While Keen claims that this element is found in one's autobiography, Moltmann asserts that this beginning point is discovered in the universal cry for freedom which extends even to the Godhead. God identifies with his creation as men, women, and nature itself suffer and call out. For the Christian, moreover, this foundational concern is given historical and definitive shape by the Cross of Jesus, where what is truly evil in the world (the torture of creation and the unredeemed condition of the world) is revealed.

Moltmann juxtaposes the questions posed by our existence and creation's (mis)use with the "*vision* proclaimed by Christian hope"—that vision of Jesus Christ and his future.[40] Based on a definite reality in history, Moltmann's concrete vision "announces the future of that reality, its future possibilities and its power over the future."[41] This vision (Christian revelation) does not merely introduce something that was always there; "rather, it makes present that which does not yet exist."[42] It does not "disclose" history or existence, as Keen would claim, allowing us to return to Eden. Rather, it "opens up" history and existence to a new horizon—the coming of God.

Contrasting with his diagnosis of the present negative aspects of life is Moltmann's theological perspective of God's future, a vision which not only provides all of life with an intentional structure but also carries with it a program for action. Given the present, God not only promises, he calls; "man" not only hopes, he plans.[43] Here is the *raison d'etre* for Moltmann's political theology: the *pro-missio* (promise) of the Kingdom becomes the clarion call for a *missio* (mission) of love. "Hope . . . mobilizes to a new obedience," writes Moltmann, for hope remains "a permanent disquiet . . . not comfort, but protest, not nightmarish enthusiasms, but resistance, suffering, not escape but love—that is what hope brings into life."[44]

Moltmann's Theology Vis-à-vis Play

Soon after Moltmann's book *The Theology of Hope* appeared in English (in 1967), reviewers questioned the seemingly ironic fact that his hopeful theology had so little to do with play and celebration. For example, Daniel Migliore wrote,

> Perhaps the crucial weakness of Moltmann's work . . . is that the hope consciousness which is described is too spartan. Little attention is given to celebration, play, and humor as the necessary companions of the struggle for a new world if this struggle is not itself to be overwhelmed by the spirit of rigidity and closedness which it seeks to overcome. In his book, Moltmann speaks very briefly of the joy of Christian hope and in a recent essay [1968] characterizes Christian hope which can laugh, but he has not yet productively explored the relation between a theology of hope and a theology of play.[45]

As if he were responding directly to his American critics, Moltmann chose as his topic for an address to the annual meeting of the American Academy of Religion in 1970 the implications of his theology of hope in regard to play.[46] In expanded and revised form, these remarks became *Theology of Play*.[47]

As one might suspect from the description of Moltmann's larger theology, play is for him highly purposeful. Moltmann believes that any critical theory of play should start with a consideration of its political function in light of our present social reality. Theories of play, when separated from play's life-context, quickly become obsolete. For Moltmann, our present cultural situation is one in which freedom has become a rarity, and with it, laughter and play. "One can only laugh in freedom," he suggests. But while our brothers starve in India and are tortured in Brazil, what freedom does any citizen of our *one* world have? Thus, in discussing play, Moltmann addresses those who grieve and protest. The inauthentic play of those who, like Keen, deceive themselves with superficial optimism is of no interest to Moltmann. "I am speaking," he says, "to those who are so oppressed by the misery of this society and by their own impotence that they would prefer to either doubt or forget."[48]

According to Moltmann, society's misery is not located only

in the world's trouble spots. It is apparent in both West Germany and America. We live in a context in which labor is losing its meaning, becoming empty. When we play, we most often use the experience as a safety valve to release the frustration of work's oppression. Unable to be truly free from our burdens, we all too often end up replaying the very same things we have endured in our work ("workers at rattling machines relax on crackling motorcycles").[49] Play in our society of compulsion and work oftentimes does little more than provide a quality of suspension, temporarily unburden us, or assist political stabilization, work morality, and social regimentation. In other words, it is seldom authentic play. Play has become alienated, bound up by the control of ruling authority. It is play without hope, serving only to make us forget what we are still not able to change.

Moltmann's *diagnosis,* then, is twofold: (1) it seems wrong to play or dance while others are suffering, and (2) play has too often become the servant of the oppressor.

Over against this diagnosis, Moltmann sets in dialectical tension his eschatological *vision* of "The Theological Play of God's Good Pleasure." It is an aesthetic vision, one that has largely been obliterated by our ethical posture toward life. Perhaps we can best perceive it, Moltmann suggests, by turning to the simple questions children are most likely to ask. "Why did God create the world? And why did God become man?" Moltmann answers by stating that in creation God "played" meaningfully and freely with his own possibilities, not needing to be productive but demonstrating the wealth of his riches joyfully, according to his own good pleasure. Similarly, there was no compelling reason for God to become man in Jesus other than that it was according to his good pleasure. Moreover, Jesus' correspondence to God's deepest nature (his "freedom which is love") allowed him his radical liberation from the "dead seriousness" of history, says Moltmann; the laughter of Easter reveals that life can indeed be taken playfully.[50]

Moltmann moves on to ask a final question, this time from the world of *Homo Faber*: "What is the ultimate purpose of history?" Christian eschatology, he answers, has a similar playful focus, i.e., it must be viewed as "totally without purpose, as a hymn of praise for unending joy, as an ever varying round dance of the redeemed in the trinitarian fullness of God, and as the complete harmony of soul and body." In other words, Christian eschatology must be painted like creation in "the colors of aesthetic categories." Moltmann's vision is of a beautiful, playful God who is bringing into being our playful future with him. In Christian theology we have overemphasized God's dominion and failed to explore the implications of God's glory. Moltmann is not suggesting that aesthetics be substituted for ethics as the focusing principle of our vision of God, but rather that these two principles be viewed as inseparable.[51]

For Moltmann, the importance of aesthetics as well as ethics holds true not only for our awareness of God but also for our derivative life of faith. Without the free play of the imagination, the Christian's rightful obedience deteriorates into legalism. This is the third part of Moltmann's dialectical theology of play—his *prescription*. Given our work-oriented suffering, unrest, and joy-less play, and given the eschatological visions both of God's playfulness and of our future as "players," it follows that we are to usher in God's future by living now "spontaneously, unselfishly, as if playing." Moltmann entitles his argument "The Human Play of Liberated Mankind."[52]

Freed by the justifying future of God from self-assertion and self-searching, the Christian is able to play. In his play the Christian shows the "demonstrative value of being" and also gives a "prevision, foretaste, and preplay" of our future with God.[53] Moltmann recognizes that existing forms of play have too often had a nonpolitical character and an a-political tendency. But this is wrong. Given our present inhumanity and God's future Kingdom, we must make the liberating effects of play "more precise and more aimed at a specific goal."[54] Play's aim should be that of "driving men to uncover their true humanity which still lies hidden in darkness."[55]

An Evaluation

At times Moltmann has been attentive and open both to the phenomenon of play and to the Christian tradition and its sources. For example, his nine pages describing play, based in a theological reflection on creation, are perceptive and honest to both Scripture and the play experience.[56] Quoting the *Westminster Catechism* of 1647, he speaks of "man's chief end" being "to glorify God and enjoy him forever." "Joy is the meaning of human life," he asserts. Moltmann even observes perceptively that for the catechism to pose its question in the way it does (What is man's chief end?) is to risk confusing "the enjoyment of God and our existence with goals and purposes."[57]

As creatures, writes Moltmann, we can celebrate our freedom amid "the endless beauties and liberties of the finite concomitants of the infinite joy of the creator." "The moral and political *seriousness of making history* and of historical struggles" can be "suspended by a *calm rejoicing in existence itself.*" In this way labor is not ignored but finds itself protected "against the demonic, against despair, against man's self-deification and self-vilification. . . ." Viewed in this light, play serves as a model for life as a whole, as we realize that God himself is playing a wondrous game with us.[58]

Unfortunately, however, Moltmann is not consistent either in centering his theological reflection on play in creation or in allowing play its aesthetic posture. All too quickly creation becomes a subset of redemption and aesthetics a subset of ethics. It is this twin and overlapping inconsistency that undermines Moltmann's theology of play, radically qualifying its usefulness for ongoing Christian reflection. Both criticisms need elaboration.

Moltmann's essay on play is entitled "The First Liberated Men in Creation," but his focus is not on creation but on eschatology. Or, to put the matter more precisely, Moltmann considers creation, but he redefines it as a backward projection in light of our eschatological hope. It was in light of the Exodus, Moltmann believes—it was in light of the God of Promise—that the Israelites were led to reflect upon their beginnings. How could the Israelites explain the discrepancy between their present suffering and their future hope? According to Moltmann, the creation story became a way of maintaining their vision, and thus another creative witness to our call and commission in the world. Seen in this light, creation theology (that biblical reflection based on life as a gift from God—e.g., the first chapter of Genesis, Proverbs, Ecclesiastes, Song of Songs, etc.) becomes merely a subset of eschatology, and as such is reduced to an impetus for mission.

For Moltmann, "The seventh day of creation is still ahead of God and his people in history." The "rest of God"—i.e., his non-work, or play, and ours—is viewed as "a promise of the end of history."[59] In this way Moltmann pushes into the future "the demonstrative joy in existence" characteristic of both play and creation theology. But this is to misread the biblical texts in order to make them serve other than their intended purposes. What is written from the perspective of fulfillment Moltmann recasts in terms of expectation. The result is that both God's pleasure (play) at the completion of his creative act and man's play at the beginning of his life as creature defined by God's graciousness fail to receive a legitimate place.

Moltmann's hermeneutical predilections for promise over fulfillment, for ethics over aesthetics, and for mission over rest also cause him to ignore play's self-contained meaning and instead to explore the *function* of play in contemporary society. Moltmann thinks that play needs to be politicized by having its liberating effect made more precise and "more clearly aimed at a specific goal."[60] In spite of his helpful vision of eschatological play, he would seek to instrumentalize play—i.e., to make conscious use of it—for the sake of the revolution.

For Moltmann, play is a form of mission. "The vocation of every lover [including the player] is to bring about revolution," he says, quoting Che Guevara.[61] But here we see clearly the deficiency of his position. The vocation of the lover (as any real lover knows) might lead to revolution, but in itself it is first and foremost *to be* a lover. And the vocation of the player is to play, to accept, to offer—not to seek change. Moltmann quickly passes over this primary experience of play to dwell on its unintended but beneficial consequences. Moltmann thinks there are three consequences, which he wishes to make intentional. First, as mission, play functions as the negation of the negative. It is the way of the clown; it is a powerful way to stand in judgment. Play is "the means the powerless use to shake off their yoke."[62] Secondly, play functions as a means of keeping the revolution human—of preventing the revolution from becoming a new form of oppression. Christian play, operating within and on behalf of the revolution of God's future, can keep us aware of our frailty by thrusting before us the humorous incongruities of life.[63] Thirdly, play functions as experimentation for and anticipation of a better future. It is "a means of testing a new life-style."[64] In play we are given a pre-vision, a foretaste of the Messianic banquet. Play is "fore-play"—preparation for our future with God.

Moltmann wants to see both creation theology and play itself through a single lens—his eschatological hope. In this way the richness of both present experience and Christian theology is flattened and reduced to the single focus of our mission of realizing God's future within our present suffering and affliction. In this framework, play does not fit easily within our present anguish, so Moltmann defines it as that proleptic experience of the future which is in God's hand, and our mission of liberation on behalf of that future. Moltmann's imperialistic future causes him to turn from his portrayal of "created" and "creative" play and reduce play to a means of liberation.

Play as Preparatory to Religion: Peter Berger and C. S. Lewis

The wild thyme unseen, or the winter lightning
Or the waterfall, or music heard so deeply
That it is not heard at all, but you are the music
While the music lasts. These are only hints and
*   guesses,*
Hints followed by guesses; and the rest
Is prayer, observance, discipline, thought and
*   action.*
The hint half guessed, the gift half understood is
*   Incarnation.*

—T. S. ELIOT[65]

Despite their profound differences, Keen and Moltmann have one thing in common: their functionally oriented theologies ultimately turn play into a form of work. However unconsciously, they prove to be students of our modern age, theologians influenced by our continuing compulsion to work. Keen would have us work at our play in order to escape the drudgery and disappointment in life; Moltmann would have us play as an alternate form of mission. For both, their preoccupation with the larger concerns of life aborts the world of play.

Thus it is not from these professional theologians that we will acquire a Christian understanding of play. Instead, fundamental insight into the Christian significance of play can better be gained from two more informal theologians, men whose primary training is outside the realm of theology and more directly related to play—the sociologist Peter Berger and the literary critic C. S. Lewis. Their occasional writings on play seem truer to the experience of play on its own terms, and so can be better incorporated into an adequate theological formulation.

In his book *A Rumor of Angels,* Peter Berger inquires into the possibility of theological thinking within our present situation. As both a sociologist and a Christian (though he admits that he has not yet found the heresy into which his theological views comfortably fit), Berger attempts to deal with the alleged demise of the supernatural in our modern world. Berger suggests that in the days ahead—unless surprises occur—we will see the continuation of the secularizing trend which is already apparent in society, though he admits that the evidence is not as all-embracing as some have thought. Berger hastens to point out, however, that although secularism is our situation, this does not shed light on the truth or falsity of the supernatural per se, but only on the seeming incapacity of our contemporaries to conceive of it. We need not feel tryannized by the present, for whether theology is a human projection or a reflection of divine realities depends upon one's initial assumptions about reality. Either conclusion is logically possible.

What our present situation suggests to Berger is not the demise of the religious but a necessary approach or methodology for theological reflection: "The theological decision will have to be that, 'in, with and under' the immense array of human projections, there are indicators of a reality that is truly 'other' and that the religious imagination of man ultimately reflects." Berger believes that the only possible starting point for theology today is the anthropological. For "if the religious projections of man correspond to a reality that is superhuman and supernatural, then it seems logical," suggests Berger, "to look for traces of this reality in the projector himself."[66]

In looking for inductive possibilities for a move from anthropology *to* theology, i.e., in attempting to find an anchorage for theology in fundamental human experience, Berger turns to our common, "universal" experiences—to what he labels "prototypical human gestures." Here he finds "what might be called *signals of transcendence* within the empirically given human situation." By this term Berger means "phenomena that are to be found within the domain of our 'natural' reality but that appear to point beyond that reality." One such phenomenon, according to Berger, is our play.[67]

Berger follows Johan Huizinga in his discussion of the person at play. When one is playing, Berger says, one is going by different time. No longer is it 11:00 a.m. as it is in the "serious" world, but it is the third round, the fourth act, or the second kiss. Moreover, when play's joyful intention is realized, the time structure of play takes on still another quality—"it becomes eternity." "Joyful play appears to suspend, or bracket, the reality of our 'living toward death' (as Heidegger aptly described our 'serious' condition)." Such transcendent joy can be interpreted as a merciful illusion, a regression to childish magic, or in an act of faith can also be understood as a "signal of transcendence." Viewed from this latter perspective, our "natural" experience of "eternity" in play is seen as pointing to its "supernatural" fulfillment. Such a reinterpretation of our play should be understood as encompassing, rather than contradicting, the explanations of empirical reason. For Berger, religion becomes the ultimate vindication of joyful play.[68]

The important point for Berger is that such faith as results from the play event is inductive, resting on the experiences of our everyday lives. According to Berger, theology need not be rooted in a mysterious revelation available only to the few; it can stem from those natural experiences generally accessible to all people. Berger believes that play carries within itself the capacity for ecstasy. That is, in play we are able to step outside the "taken-for-granted reality of everyday life" and open ourselves up to the mystery that surrounds us on all sides. Play has a transcendent dimension, though it is important to note that this theological rootage is found not in the mystical or extraordinary but in a basic experience common to all.

Berger believes that his "anthropological starting point" will be "intrinsically repulsive to most conservative forms of theology." But this is not necessarily the case. C. S. Lewis, for example, with whom many conservative theologians readily identify, agrees with much of what Berger sets forth, as I will suggest below. His theological difference with Berger would come not with Berger's starting with human experience but with his desire to end there. Berger reasons that "in any empirical frame of reference, transcendence must appear as a projection of man. Therefore, if transcendence is to be spoken of *as* transcendence, the empirical frame of reference must be left behind." And this is something Berger the theologian, as well as Berger the sociologist, is unwilling to do.[69]

Berger wishes to speak of "a God who is not made by man, who is outside and not within ourselves," but he limits his act of faith in such a God to projections outward from common human experience, i.e., to signals of transcendence.[70] The result is that Berger is left finally with his *own* experience alone, a consequence that weakens his understanding not only of Christian theology but ultimately of play as well. Regarding Christian theology, Berger is left without outside confirmation for his suggestive experiences of play, the authority of Scripture being effectively denied. As he himself admits, what he has is "hypothesis," not "proclamation."[71] Moreover, regarding play, Berger is reduced to a hope, a "rumor" that his transcendent experiences are indeed what they seem, dialogical, or "co-relational," humankind in fact being met by the divine.

Berger has been both perceptive and consistent in his description of play, and his observations about the possible religious dimensions of this sphere of cultural activity are suggestive. But Berger's propensity to expound theology solely on an empirical, inductive basis—his desire, that is, to make anthropology not only the starting point but the continuing locus of his theology—actually results in a diminished play experience as well as a truncated Christianity. It is Berger's larger theological hermeneutics, not his "anthropological starting point," which traditional Christian theologians will challenge.[72]

Play can indeed prove helpful as a starting point for Christian theology, but it need not be described only from the standpoint of the projecting player, nor should it be thought the final word. Our human reach toward the transcendent can be met by God's outstretched arm breaking into history. Open to the divine through play, the modern person can continue on to experience the reality of God through his special revelation centering in the Exodus and in Jesus Christ. Inductive faith can provide a prolegomena for deductive faith, but it cannot serve as the totality of the Christian gospel. There needs to be a circulation between theological induction and theological deduction.

In his autobiography, *Suprised by Joy,* C. S. Lewis describes several play experiences of his childhood and youth in which he was pointed to something beyond the ordinary horizons of our world, in which he was opened outward to the transcendent. The first such experience occurred when he was six, as he gazed at a toy garden that his brother made for him out of moss, decorated with twigs and flowers, and set in the lid of a biscuit tin. In the years that followed, he heard play's voice of Joy when he smelled a flowering currant bush, when he discovered the autumn of Beatrix Potter's *Squirrel Nutkin,* when he read Longfellow's *Saga of King Olaf,* and again when he later became involved in Wagnerian Romanticism.

Lewis had continuing difficulty defining or even describing these experiences of "Joy." For him, Joy was distinct from mere happiness on the one hand, and from aesthetic pleasure on the other. He thought that authentic Joy was characterized by "the stab, the pang, the inconsolable longing" that was aroused. Joy was highly "desirable" in two senses of that word, its winsomeness residing in the desire it called forth. Furthermore, this Joy could not be sought directly, for it came "more externally" as the participant gave his whole attention to his experience of play. In describing this experience of Joy, Lewis was attempting to circumscribe that non-sought-after result of play which we have described as play's proclivity to open one outward to the transcendent.[73]

This Joy—"this pointer to something other and outer," as Lewis described it—was something Lewis knew primarily as a distant longing until he chanced to pick up at a bookstall George MacDonald's *Phantastes, a Faerie Romance.* As he read this book, he was changed:

> It was as though the voice which had called to me from the world's end were now speaking at my side. It was, with me in the room, or in my body, or behind me. If it had once eluded me by its distance, it now eluded me by proximity—something too near to see, too plain to be understood, on this side of knowledge.

Lewis goes on to relate: "That night my imagination was, in a certain sense, baptized; the rest of me, not unnaturally took longer. I had not the faintest notion what I had let myself in for by buying *Phantastes.*"[74]

Lewis reflected often upon the meaning of his "baptism of the imagination" through play. According to Lewis, modern man lives in a tiny windowless universe, his boundaries narrowed to too small a focus.[75] Through such play experiences as the reading of stories—when one could experience life "in a sense 'for fun,' and with [his] feet on the fender"—Lewis believed that modern man could perhaps recapture a sense of his distant horizons, much as he once had.[76] For Lewis, a story was the embodiment of, or mediation of, the "more." Plot was important, for example, but only as "a net whereby to catch something else." This something added was not an escape from reality, thought Lewis, though it was a reality baffling to the intellect. "It may not be 'like real life' in the superficial sense," Lewis stated, "but it sets before us an image of what reality may well be like at some more central region."[77] For example, when children read about enchanted woods, they do not begin to despise the real woods. Rather, "the reading makes all real woods a little enchanted."[78]

According to Lewis, a good story (and authentic play experiences more generally) has a mythic quality:

> It arouses in us sensations we have never had before, never anticipated having as though we had broken out of our normal mode of consciousness and possess joys ["Joy"] not promised to our birth! It gets under our skin, hits us at a level deeper than our thoughts or even our passions, troubles oldest certainties till all questions are reopened, and in general shocks us more fully awake than we are for most of our lives.[79]

Lewis realized that there is no guarantee that a given story will cause a given reader to respond in this way. But as the story is encountered playfully, its myth-making potential can perhaps be actualized. For Lewis, his experience with MacDonald's *Phantastes* had been such a mythic event. It had surprised him with Joy.

Lewis thought that one's play experiences offered the possibility of being transformed by Joy as one entered fully into the play event. In play, Joy's "bright shadow" might reveal to the participant that indefinite, yet real, horizon of meaning beyond his normally perceived world.[80] In play one sometimes glimpses pre-critically ("on this side of knowledge") a more ultimate reality as he breaks out of his "normal modes of consciousness."[81]

In Lewis's view, however, Joy is not only the player's experience. It is also a voice "from the world's end" calling him — also "that of which Joy is the desiring."[82] Not only do we "enjoy," but God, who is Lewis's ultimate reality, expresses his Joy toward us. Moreover, God's expression of Joy is not limited to the expression of play. Play having opened him up to the possibility of relating directly to Joy itself, Lewis later found that Joy to be fully actualized in his personal experience with Jesus Christ.[83] According to Lewis, not only does God's Joy cause us to "en-joy" on the tangent of play's horizon where the radical otherness of God meets the radical wholeness of humankind, but Joy also expresses itself in the encounter with the person of Christ. Only through this second experience of Joy did Lewis fully recognize Joy's "bright shadow" for what it was: "holiness."[84] Lewis ends *Surprised by Joy* by relating, very simply, this second-order experience of Joy: "I was driven to Whipsnade one sunny morning. When we set out I did not believe that Jesus Christ was the Son of God, and when we reached the zoo I did."[85] Surprised once by Joy in his play, Lewis was open to other, more definite experiences of Joy.

Play's potential for "holiness" became a life-long concern for Lewis. Particularly in his imaginative literature — in his allegories, children's novels, and space triology — it proved both a motivation and a recurring theme. What MacDonald had done for him, he hoped to do for his readers. For example, in his science-fiction novel, *Out of the Silent Planet,* Lewis wrote of Elwin Ransom, a Cambridge philologist who is kidnapped and taken to another planet. At the end of the story (and the story is a good one), Lewis adds a postscript. The narrator states, "It is time to remove the mask and to acquaint the reader with the real and practical purpose for which this book has been written." He then relates how Ransom himself suggested, after his return to earth, that they "publish in the form of *fiction* what would certainly not be listened to as fact." As Ransom explained it: "What we need for the moment is not so much a body of belief as a body of people familiarized with certain ideas. If we could even effect in one per cent of our readers a change-over from the conception of Space to the conception of Heaven, we should have made a beginning."[86] What happened to Ransom is what happened to Lewis himself. Ransom now saw "space" as "heaven." It was not a "black, cold vacuity" but an "empyrean ocean of radiance."[87] What he discovered he desired all to know.

A second allusion to Lewis's own story is found in *The Pilgrim's Regress,* when Lewis portrays John hearing these words near the Canyon: "For this end I made your senses and for this end your imagination that you might see My face and live."[88] Similarly, in *The Lion, the Witch and the Wardrobe,* Lucy first discovers Narnia while playing in a wardrobe. When the other children ridicule her for claiming to have been in an-"other world," the wise professor chides them for not believing her testimony:

> 'Logic!' said the Professor half to himself. 'Why don't they teach logic at these schools? There are only three possibilities. Either your sister is telling lies, or she is mad, or she is telling the truth. You know she doesn't tell lies and it is obvious that she is not mad. For the moment then and unless any further evidence turns up, we must assume that she is telling the truth.'[89]

At the end of the fantasy, after all the children have "played" their way into Narnia and returned the wiser, they ask the professor if they can't return to Narnia by the same route. Again the professor speaks for Lewis:

> 'You won't get into Narnia again by *that* route. . . . Eh? What's that? Yes, of course you'll get back to Narnia again some day. Once a King in Narnia, always a King in Narnia. . . . Indeed, don't *try* to get there at all. It'll happen when you're not looking for it. . . . Bless me, what *do* they teach them at these schools.'[90]

The players cannot manipulate their experiences to make them produce the numinous. They can only play, suggests Lewis, confident that Joy will come in its own season.

To give a final example, in *The Voyage of the Dawn Treader,* Lewis portrays the children sailing to the end of the world, hoping to reach the land of Aslan the lion. They finally come to that place where the earth meets the sky, and they wade ashore. Meeting a dazzlingly white lamb, they ask how they can get into Aslan's country. The lamb answers that they reach that place from their own world: " 'There is a way into my country from all the worlds,' said the Lamb; but as he spoke his snowy white flushed into tawny gold and his size changed and he was Aslan himself, towering above them and scattering light from his mane." Aslan tells them that in their world " 'I have another name. You must learn to know me by that name. This was the very reason why you were brought to Narnia, that by knowing me here for a little, you may know me better there.' "[91]

The preceding description of Berger's and Lewis's positions should have made clear their differing views on play's "religious" impulse, but the difference is important enough to be reiterated. For here is one basic distinction that can be drawn between various theologies of play. Can theology be built solely out of certain natural experiences (like play) which are generally accessible to all people? Or is God's redeeming presence in the world, including his relationship with us as players, finally fully known only as it is experienced in his engendering relationship with us through Jesus Christ? Is it enough to believe that play's "signal" is rooted in God? Is it enough to hear "a rumor of angels"? Or is such "Joy" adequately known only through God's self-definition in Jesus Christ?

We noted that Berger admits that for him to speak of play's transcendent dimension as transcendence is an act of *personal* faith. Berger believes, however, that such faith needs to be limited to projections outward from our common experiences and must rest at the stage of hypothesis. Lewis, on the other hand, is somewhat bolder in drawing implications from the "transcendent" dimension of play. Play need not surprise an individual with Joy, but it can. Furthermore, God's subsequent definition of himself in Jesus Christ allows Lewis the hindsight to call his experience of Joy in play an experience of the holy. Play's transcendent dimension, its experience of the meeting of the holy and the human spirit, is fully understood *as* transcendence only in light of the Spirit's further definitive work on Lewis's behalf, his introduction of Lewis to the person of Christ. Here the Spirit heard in play and the Spirit of Christ are seen to be one and the same. As Walter Hooper, Lewis's literary executor, rightly observes, "In Lewis the natural and the supernatural seemed to be one, to flow one into the other."[92]

By allowing us to transcend ourselves and enter a new time

and space, play can become the avenue through which God communes with us. This is what the children in Lewis's Narnia tales discovered. In its push toward communion with others, play can be the context wherein one is first met by the Other. As the human spirit freely gives itself in the search for kindred spirits, i.e., for "I-Thou" relationships, that experience can be serendipitously transformed by the Holy Spirit. Thus play can become an encounter with the Holy. Seen in this way, listening to Mozart can be a theologically significant event, as it was for Barth—though it need not be. And reading Ignazio Silone's novels is the opportunity to hear God speak pseudonymously, as it was for Robert McAfee Brown. And imagining the fantasy worlds of George MacDonald can result in being "surprised by Joy," as it did for Lewis. Like Lewis, I do not want to compromise either God's freedom or the "purposelessness" of play by suggesting a necessary relationship between our play and the divine encounter. Rather, it is enough to suggest that in play God can, and often does, meet us and commune with us. The result is a new openness to the religious more generally, our experience of the sacred in play serving as a prolegomenon to further encounters with God.

What can be said to conclude this survey of present theological options open to the Christian at play? Should we, as Sam Keen would suggest, turn play into a total ideology, a new agenda, an alternate "work" strategy? Should we as Christians baptize that counterculture of self-fulfillers which Yankelovich documents so well? The result might well prove to be even more destructive both of our personhoods and of society's well-being than our present externally directed work agenda. Such romanticizing of life's possibilities runs roughshod over a necessary Christian realism. We are not to fiddle while Rome burns! On the other hand, we must also beware lest we reduce play to merely another political agenda. Play takes priority over all such programming. It is part of our God-intended humanity.

For the last part of his life, Dietrich Bonhoeffer wrote from the horror of his World War II prison cell, fully recognizing the serious political agenda he was committed to. Nevertheless, he had this to say about play in a letter to his friends Eberhard and Renate Bethge:

> I wonder whether it is possible (it almost seems so today) to regain the idea of the *Church* as providing an understanding of the area of freedom (art, education, friendship, play), so that Kierkegaard's "aesthetic existence" would not be banished from the Church's sphere, but would be reestablished within it? I really think so. . . . Who is there, for instance, in our times, who can devote himself with an easy mind to music, friendship, games, or happiness? Surely not the "ethical" man but only the Christian.[93]

The player who plots, even if it is for God and neighbor, is no longer playing. Play is not for the sake of anything else. It is part of that "area of freedom" which has its own justification, even in the most dire of times. And here C. S. Lewis can assist us in our understanding. If we would but play, we might be surprised by the Joy of God himself. True, there is no guarantee that Joy will occur. But God has made us creatures with the capacity for communion with him, not only in and through our work but also in and through our play. And in a time when work is proving increasingly sterile and defective, could it not be through our play that the serendipity of God's presence might most easily be experienced?

IV

Play:
A Biblical Model

GIVEN THE CENTRAL PLACE OF PLAY IN THE LIVES OF
all people—given the fact that we do some things as ends in
themselves without ulterior motive or outside design, freely entering into such activity within its own time (a playtime) and its
own space (a playground) and its own order (a playbook)—it
is surprising that we understand play so poorly. Surprising, too,
is the fact that the Christian Church has put so little thought
into the person at play. Rather than ground their discussion in
biblical reflection and careful observation of play itself, Christians have most often been content to allow Western culture to
shape their understanding of the human at play.

At the risk of oversimplification, one can see that the two
major approaches toward play which have dominated our culture also characterize the Church's attitudes. (There are basic
affinities here with the theologies of Sam Keen and Jurgen Moltmann, although the analogy should not be overdrawn.) The one
tradition might best be labeled the "Greek," and the other, the
"Protestant." Both models have definitions of play shaped in
terms of work. While in the first (the "Greek") play is valued
because it is opposed to work, in the second (the "Protestant")
work is valued because it is opposed to play. The first looks to
play for that which is truly human; the other finds in work
humankind's true glory.

Before attempting to describe a biblically based alternative
(the "Hebraic" model) to these cultural models, one more in
line with the inductive play of Peter Berger and C. S. Lewis, let
us summarize these common, though inadequate, understandings.

The "Greek" Model

For the Greek citizen of old, leisure and play were what
were truly worthwhile, while the workaday world was viewed

with disdain. Work was carried out largely through a system of slaves, so that the privilege of play and the obligation of work were mutually exclusive social functions performed by two distinct groups in society. This classical view of play still retains advocates today. Josef Pieper, for example, views the world of work as "the weariness of daily labour" and desires humankind to be transported out of this "into an unending holiday."[1] Similarly, William Sadler, who agrees with Schiller's statement that "Man is only a man when he plays," states, "To live creatively means first of all to play."[2] Somehow life is reduced to an either/or—either we work and suffer spiritual and sensual anemia, or we play in order to realize our full humanity.

In the late 1960's and early 1970's, a theology of play surfaced in some sectors of the Christian Church that adopted this "Greek" model. Realizing that the world of work too often proved to be debilitating, enthusiasts of play argued for play's centrality in human existence. Lawrence Meredith, for example, rhapsodized about the possibilities of play over work in his book *The Sensuous Christian*:

> Perhaps day after tomorrow, by some miracle of ecological awareness, food *will* just be. Then the psychedelic path will lead over the bridge of cybernation; and with Herbert Marcuse as guru emeritus, Norman O. Brown as classicist in residence, and William F. Buckley, Jr., as anti-utopian court jester, we will establish the new-consciousness Camelot, telling the little ones tales of old Greenwich Village, the Haight, Millbrook, the Peanut Butter Conspiracy, of all the lotus-eating cadres of the leisure class. . . . The university could, in fact, become what it was: a *playground* and not a battleground. The church everywhere could be a happening where joy is like the rain.[3]

Meredith's utopia is, of course, an unintentional parody of the world of play he desires, for Greenwich Village and the Haight have proven to be anything but precursors of Camelot. But like Sam Keen and other theologians of play, Meredith is instructive, for he presents—hyperbolically, perhaps—one paradigm of the Christian at play.

The "Protestant" Model

Although this "Greek" model has a growing list of modern-day proponents, both inside and outside the Church, the more dominant tradition regarding play remains the "Protestant." In this model, industry, individualism, frugality, ambition, and success are considered the primary virtues, with work being understood as the criterion by which a life is judged successful. Within this model, an unfortunate diminishment of the play experience occurs. Play is conceived of as time off from work, and thus time vulnerable to misuse. Whereas for the "Greek," play is the perfect human state, for the "Protestant" play is merely a reward for past work, a temptation to idleness, or a pause that refreshes. Margaret Mead notes that "within traditional American culture . . . there runs a persistent belief that all leisure [play] must be earned by work and good works . . . [and] second, while it is enjoyed it must be seen in a context of future work and good works."[4] Play is, it seems, reduced to the poor stepchild of work. It is the alter side, that which stands behind, that which issues from work and finds its ultimate justification not in itself but in the work already or yet to be accomplished.

Within the Church are many modern-day advocates of this "Protestant" perspective on play. Rudolph Norden, for example, in his book *The Christian Encounters the New Leisure,* argues that for the Christian, leisure is that time which should serve the family welfare; that time in which worship takes place; or that time which relieves tension. He would have us read more *good* books, write letters, check the family budget, sew, work in the workshop, visit friends, or pursue any number of other "excellent leisure pastimes." For Norden, play is valid only as long as it is purposeful for something beyond itself.[5]

The "Hebraic" Model

The central problem for the Christian player in America today is nicely summarized by Bennett Berger. "We are all," he writes, "at least in principle, compromised Greek citizens carrying the burden of compromised Protestant ethics."[6] It is this spiritual and emotional burden, this cultural ambivalence, that influences most Christian discussion of play and hinders many of us from allowing play its God-intended place. Christian theology, if it is to be *Christian* theology, must do more than simply acquiesce to its surrounding culture. Theology, if it is to explore adequately the meaning of play and its relation to the sacred, must "study the various biblical traditions and engage in the systematic hermeneutical task of appropriating the meaning of the biblical message for today's world."[7] These are the words of Gregory Baum in his critique of Peter Berger, and they aptly state the issue we must now turn to. What is a biblical understanding of play?

Such a question has seldom been addressed. When it has, the answers have too often seemed meager, if not counterproductive. For example, in his *Essentials of Bible History*, Elmer Mould writes of play:

> The Hebrews were a serious people; yet there are many hints of an innate lightheartedness and readiness to play when they had a chance. Children played in the streets [Zech. 8:5]. Weddings, the harvest festivals, and the religious feasts were the only holidays for adults. Jer. 31:12f. characterizes the holiday mood. Most of this play seems to have been impromptu. . . .[8]

Mould goes on to describe a set of backgammon pieces that was found in the excavation of Tell Beit Mirsim Kiriath-sepher at the level of 1600 B.C. He comments, "It is not an idle play of fancy to think of the biblical Hebrews playing the . . . game." He then concludes, "No doubt the most common form of amusement was exchanging stories."[9] Mould's comments are suggestive but contain more surmise than solid evidence.

A second example comes from Alan Richardson's often helpful study of *The Biblical Doctrine of Work*. He writes:

> The Bible knows nothing of "a problem of leisure." No such problem had in fact arisen in the stage of social evolution which had been reached in biblical times. The hours of daylight were the hours of labour for all workers (cf. Ps. 104.22f., John 9.4), whose only leisure-time was during the hours of darkness. The general standpoint of the Bible is that it is "folly" (i.e., sinful) to be idle between daybreak and sunset. A six- or an eight-hour day was not envisaged. Hence we must not expect to derive from the Bible any explicit guidance upon the right use of leisure.[10]

If the Hebrews were, in fact, a "serious people" who viewed leisure as "folly" or at best an "impromptu" respite, then the "systematic hermeneutical task of appropriating the meaning of the biblical message [concerning play] for today's world" would be difficult, if not impossible. We would need to ask whether the term "Christian player" is not a self-contradiction. But such is not the case. Rather, our cultural bias toward work and the Bible's primary concern with God's "work" of salvation have blinded traditional critics to the biblical discussions of play that are in fact present.

There is a section of the Scriptures that is not as concerned with God's saving acts in history as with God the creator involved in history. Here—in Genesis 1-11, in the Sabbath ordinance, in Proverbs, Ecclesiastes, and the Song of Songs—we find a God concerned with our play as well as our work, our aesthetics as well as our ethics. Here the intended shape of created life is described and illustrated. For example, God is said to have "made every tree that is *pleasant* to the sight and *good* for food" (Gen. 2:9). Commenting on this passage, Leland Ryken writes: "Mankind's perfect environment, in other words, satisfies a dual criterion, both aesthetic and utilitarian. The conditions for human well-being have never changed from that moment in Paradise. People live by beauty as well as truth."[11] Or perhaps, to paraphrase Ryken loosely, we could say that people live by "play" as well as by "work."

God need not have created a world that is beautiful as well as functional. But he did, as the Psalmist reiterates:

> Thou dost cause the grass to grow for the cattle,
>   and plants for man to cultivate,
> that he may bring forth food from the earth,
>   and wine to gladden the heart of man,
> oil to make his face shine,
>   and bread to strengthen man's heart. (Ps. 104: 14, 15)

God has planted crops for our sustenance—to produce wine, oil, and bread (grain). His work (creation) and ours (cultivation) produce that food necessary to strengthen one's total being (Heb. "heart"). But note that the explanation extends beyond the functional or the utilitarian. The bread will strengthen us, but the wine is to gladden our hearts and the oil to make our faces shine. Elsewhere in the Bible, oil can have a protective function (cf. Deut. 28:40; Ps. 92:10), but this is not the purpose the Psalmist mentions. Rather, the oil is a sign of gladness and celebration (cf. Ps. 23:5, 45:7; Prov. 27:9; Isa. 61:3). Similarly, the wine is valued not simply because it slakes one's thirst or increases physical vitality; it gladdens the "heart," i.e., life itself (cf. Judg. 9:13; Eccl. 10:19).

It is this "Hebraic" perspective on creation that gives the Christian theologian insight into play in today's world. Here is a viewpoint concerning our play (and our work) alternate to that found in much of contemporary society: (1) It can be heard in the discussion of Sabbath rest; (2) It is basic to the advice offered by Ecclesiastes; (3) It is pervasive in the sexuality of the Song of Songs; (4) It is played out in such Israelite practices as festival, dance, feasting, and the providing of hospitality to travelers; (5) Although somewhat harder to demonstrate textually, it is even central to the pattern of Jesus' friendships.

1. The Rest of the Sabbath

Of all the various Old Testament instructions, none is more central to Israelite life than the law of the Sabbath. Not only does it take up more space in the Decalogue than any of the other commandments, but it is reformulated and discussed throughout the pages of Scripture. Whether the Sabbath originated with the Israelites themselves or whether Israel appropriated within her Yahwistic context practices from surrounding cultures need not concern us here. (The Babylonian *shappatu* and the Kenites' cultic prohibition of smiths working every seventh day are two frequently noted parallels.) What is significant for our present discussion is that Sabbath-keeping was so uniform in Israelite life that it became almost the trademark of Jewish faith and practice. By the time of the Maccabees, for example, the practice of keeping the Sabbath was so central to Judaism that, according to Josephus, the Romans had to exempt the Jews from military service because they were useless as soldiers on the Sabbath.[12] Seneca could not understand the Sabbath exercise and chided the Jews for spending every seventh day of their lives in idleness.[13]

From its inception, the Sabbath was characterized by one practice—a cessation from all physical labor. Hans Walter Wolff, writing on "The Day of Rest in the Old Testament," comments: "But how is the 'Sabbath for Yahweh' to be 'remembered,' 'observed,' 'sanctified'? The unambiguous, sole answer is: 'You shall not do any work.' "[14] Wolff theorizes on the prehistory of the Sabbath commandment, agreeing with A. Alt that "originally the Sabbath was characterized merely by the prohibition of all work, and in Israel's history had nothing to do with specific cultic worship of Yahweh as such."[15] For the twentieth-century Christian, the Sabbath is inextricably associated with worship and cult. This, however, ought to be a secondary association. Originally the Sabbath was not a time for the cult. Sacrifices were, after all, a daily event. It was first and foremost a time to abstain from work (cf. Exod. 16:22f.). It was that "parenthesis" in life which had no outside design. According to our description in Chapter Two, it was intended to be an instance of "play."

Although the Sabbath was characterized by its "strike" against all work, it would be wrong to assume, as Seneca did, that it was superfluous or useless. Like play in general, its non-instrumentality proved productive. By regularly resting from their efforts, the Israelites both found themselves refreshed and were able to renew themselves and to recall their God.

The Sabbath's recreative function has often been noted. After six days in which "man [went] forth to his work and to his labor until the evening" (Ps. 104:22), everyone in society needed refreshment, whether son or daughter, manservant or maidservant, sojourner or resident; even animals needed respite. In a break from the typical pattern of ancient Near Eastern life, the Hebrews recognized that the oppressiveness of work needed to be periodically relieved. And so it was that contrary to the "Greek" model, which allowed leisure only to the elite, and contrary to the "Protestant" model, which gloried in work-as-vocation, the "Hebraic" model declared that life was best served when all humankind both worked and then refrained from work ("played").

But the Sabbath was not only for humankind's "re-creation" (recreation?). Its focus was not only on men and women and their possibilities. It was also meant as a "demonstration" on behalf of Yahweh himself. It is in this sense that Gerhard Von Rad speaks of the Sabbath as a day which by its very nature belonged to God.[16] The Sabbath was a remembrance that Israel rested ultimately in God's graciousness. Just as the Lord instituted the Sabbath day for his people who were wandering in the wilderness, as a tangible reminder that the manna they gathered was a gift from God and not a result of their own effort (Exod.

16:22-30), so the Sabbath became a periodic reminder that one could not master life by his own effort.

In characterizing the twofold significance of the Sabbath as we have — that it is based in who we are, creatures in need of re-creation, and in who God is, one worthy of our adoration — we have reversed the historic order of justification given to the Sabbath in Scripture, although we have been true to most subsequent discussion of this biblical theme. This is important to note, particularly in an age given to defining everything vis-à-vis the human and his work experience. It is true, as W. Gunther Plaut observes, that the Sabbath "became social time devoted to the liberation of every man from the fetters of work, a liberation which included the freeman as well as the slave." But Plaut is also correct in noting that prior to this "humanization" of the Sabbath — prior to understanding the Sabbath according to its re-creative possibilities — the Sabbath was viewed simply as "God's time, the God who created the world and also created Israel."[17] Even today, when the Jew lifts his Kaddish cup on the Sabbath, he first and foremost remembers the God of Creation and the Exodus experience. It was the proclamation of God's glory, not the need for human restoration, that was the original intention of the Sabbath command.

Although the Ten Commandments given in Exodus 20 are almost identical to the record of them found in Deuteronomy 5, the Sabbath commandment is a marked exception. One can only speculate about the reasons for the differences — perhaps the changing social condition caused the Deuteronomic account to shift from a focus on God to a stronger emphasis on the human need for relief from the oppressive reality of much of work. (God's Word is always culturally directed.) But whatever the reason, these two fundamentally different descriptions and justifications for one's non-work on the Sabbath found their way successively into the inspired biblical texts. In the Decalogue given in Deuteronomy 5, we read:

> " 'Observe the Sabbath day, to keep it holy, as the Lord your God commanded you. Six days you shall labor, and do all your work; but the seventh day is a Sabbath to the Lord your God; in it you shall not do any work, you, or your son, or your daughter, or your manservant, or your maidservant . . . that your manservant and your maidservant may rest as well as you. You shall remember

that you were a servant in the land of Egypt, and the Lord your God brought you out thence with a mighty hand and an outstretched arm; therefore the Lord your God commanded you to keep the Sabbath day.' " (vv. 12-15)

In the Exodus 20 recounting of the Decalogue, however, the prior theological rationale is expressed:

"Remember the Sabbath day, to keep it holy. Six days you shall labor, and do all your work; but the seventh day is a Sabbath to the Lord your God; in it you shall not do any work . . . for in six days the Lord made heaven and earth, the sea, and all that is in them, and rested the seventh day; therefore the Lord blessed the Sabbath day and hallowed it." (vv. 8-11)

These alternate accounts base their admonition on differing motivations. Appeals to both salvation history (redemption theology) and creation theology are given as the *raison d'etre* for the Sabbath rest.

According to the Deuteronomic account, because God had delivered his people from bondage in Egypt, they were *commanded* to "play." The Hebrew term *shamor* ("*observe* the Sabbath day") has a clear ethical cast. The people are to *obey* their God by ceasing all labor. It is interesting to note that included in this version of the fourth commandment is the further ethical justification "that your manservant and your maidservant may rest as well as you." In the alternate and prior version of the Decalogue, however, an aesthetic context is suggested for the Sabbath, humankind "remembering" the Sabbath for God had *blessed* and hallowed it. The Hebrew term is *zachor*. Furthermore, it is not God's activity in the Exodus which is to be recalled but his pattern in creation, when he rested after six days of work. This "daring" (Buber) and "massive" (E. Jenni) anthropomorphism—i.e., God himself resting—perhaps finds its analogue in the communion experienced between humankind and God in the Sabbath event.[18] From their experience of Sabbath rest, the biblical writers were able to reflect (*analogia fidei*) upon the character of God himself, whom they now understood to have also "rested." Here is the context in which the meaning of the divine rest in Genesis 2 can also be understood: the point is not that God found renewed strength for his labor but rather that he stopped working.

From this brief discussion of the Sabbath emerge several

implications relevant to our discussion of play. First, the Sabbath's original intention was to qualify the Israelites' workaday world, and thus to encourage them to recognize that life was a gift as well as a task. As Alfred de Quervain points out, "Activity which can be interrupted is thereby made relative."[19] And this is as true today as ever. For those who would become lost in the intoxication of creative work (for the doctor or professor or farmer who works joyously), the play of the Sabbath is a reminder that we cannot find ultimate meaning by mastering life. As Barth suggests, "The aim of the Sabbath commandment is that man shall give and allow the omnipotent grace of God to have the first and last word at every point."[20] Our worth as God's creatures is not to be judged by the zealousness or success of our effort but by our relationship to God (cf. Neh. 13:15-22). By calling into question our single-mindness, the Sabbath—and all play analogously—serves to open us up for communion with the divine.

It is this emphasis on divine fellowship that seems to undergird the thinking of the writer of the book of Hebrews concerning Sabbath rest. The intended communion between the Creator and his creatures has been interrupted by disobedience, he argues. The result has been humankind's inability to enter fully into God's rest, i.e., to enjoy perfect fellowship with him. For this reason, the writer of Hebrews counsels: "Let us therefore strive to enter that rest. . . . let us hold fast our confession. . . . Let us then with confidence draw near to the throne of grace, that we may receive mercy and find grace to help in time of need" (Heb. 4:11-16). The writer holds out that eschatological hope that what is partial now will one day be made complete, the people of God entering fully into his rest.

Secondly, the Sabbath came to be viewed as having *ethical* significance. The Old Testament laws of the Sabbath emphasized that all servants and laborers were to rest, so that they could be refreshed (Exod. 23:12). What was at stake here was even more than a humanitarian principle, because the animals were also mentioned (surely a concern not common to other peoples in the ancient Near East; cf. Deut. 5:14). The whole of creation was seen as in travail—it was laboring—and in need of recreation. For those few today whose work is intoxicating, whose labor is more "play" than toil, the Sabbath *relativizes* their efforts. They are not to think themselves God. But for the many for whom work is wearisome, if not debilitating, the Sabbath is meant to *restore*. They are not to think themselves apart from God.

It is this recognition of the Sabbath's orientation toward the needy that causes Isaiah to connect fasting and delighting in the Sabbath with feeding the hungry from one's own supply (Isa. 58:1-14).[21] It is this same connection between Sabbath rest and human restoration that Jesus recognized, as he did not let the Sabbath stop him from collecting needed food (Mark 2:23-28), from restoring a man's withered hand (Matt. 12:9-14), or from healing a chronically ill woman (Luke 13:10-17). Whether it be rest from unrest, refreshment from drudgery, or release from endless competition, the Sabbath exists to serve humankind as much today as in Jesus' day. The circumstances have changed, but the need to turn from one's work and be refreshed remains.

The Sabbath is meant as a time of rest from the world—a period of non-work and delight in which one's "useless" activity both fosters a recognition of the divine and sanctifies and refreshes ongoing life. Described in this way, the Sabbath can be understood as analogous to, if not paradigmatic of, play as we have discussed it in Chapter Two. The Sabbath, as "play," is that parenthesis in life which has its rightful limits. Nonproductive in design, it nevertheless has significant value for its participants. Entered into freely and joyfully, it has its rules and order for the sake of its integrity. (When, as in Jesus' day, the rules became more important than the player, the Sabbath ceased to be play. But at its best, even in Jesus' day, the rules were for the sake of playing the "game.") Lastly, this "play" of the Sabbath frees one up more generally for a "playful" life-style. One's six days of work are transformed and put into perspective by the Sabbath experience.

I have compared the nature of the Sabbath with that of play not to enter into a discussion of the Sabbath practice in any further detail but rather to better focus our inquiry into its theological rationale as set forth in Scripture. For the Sabbath has been often misunderstood by Christian theologians. Alfred de Quervain, for example, in his influential discussion of the Sabbath, *Die Heiligung*, makes the point that in Israel the Sabbath was the sign of the covenant. The Israelite who did not joyfully rest from his work on that day was one who put his hope in his own work rather than in God's election.[22] According to de Quervain, ". . . when our minds are illumined by faith, we see the Sabbath in Israel as grounded not in a sociological event, but in a theological one, the deliverance of God's people from bondage into the rest which he gave them as a token of the final rest."[23]

Karl Barth draws a similar conclusion, linking the meaning of the holy day to "salvation history and its eschatological significance." While claiming that the whole of creation has as its very structure the Sabbath principle, Barth qualifies this statement by suggesting that creation (through its culmination in the Sabbath rest) points also to redemptive history (to covenant) and to the final consummation of the same. The meaning of the Sabbath for Barth thus lies in the fact that it is an "indication of the special history of the covenant and salvation," even if in a hidden form.[24] (Can we not find a preview of Moltmann's theology of play here?)[25] The Sabbath not only relativizes (or puts into proper perspective) our own workdays by actualizing the holy and securing fellowship between Yahweh and his people; it also relates us to our final day of rest. Barth quotes de Quervain approvingly at this point: "The joy of Sabbath is . . . superabundant joy at the blessings which have already been given and joy in expectation of new acts of God, of the coming salvation."[26] For Barth, the meaning and basis of the Sabbath is thus also eschatological, for by pointing to the special history of the covenant and salvation, the Sabbath necessarily points to its ultimate consummation in history.[27]

Both de Quervain and Barth (and we could add Moltmann as well) are in one sense correct. The Sabbath, like all else in the Christian faith, has a covenantal reference. But they read the Sabbath too exclusively in terms of their covenant theology. The result is that its meaning is pushed undialectically forward into the future. Although Barth refers in his Sabbath discussion to Exodus 20 and not to Deuteronomy 5, his argument ignores the Exodus account's base in creation theology. Instead, it centers almost exclusively in "salvation history." The theological events (rooted in the past and future) of the deliverance of God's people and their promise of ultimate rest (the Exodus and the coming of Christ) overshadow the present "sociological" event of the practice of the Sabbath rest itself. In the process the Sabbath's ability to recall the goodness of God in creation is lost sight of. The sociological event of the Sabbath has its theological grounds not first of all in God's past and future but in the present experience itself. For in the act of Sabbath rest, the Israelite experienced his God as a God whose very nature was one of rest. Like Moltmann, Barth and de Quervain have emphasized the frame for the play experience (past fulfillment and future promise) rather than focusing sufficiently upon the picture itself (the present experience of Sabbath "play").

Perhaps my differences with these theologians can be further clarified by Paul Jewett, who follows Barth and de Quervain on this point. Basing his hermeneutic on Oscar Cullmann's analysis of the biblical pattern of event and interpretation, new event and reinterpretation, he says:

> Applying this hermeneutic to the specific question of the Sabbath, we might say: The first event is the Exodus of the Israelites out of Egypt (Exod. 12ff.); the interpretation of this event is that God thereby delivered his people from the toil of Egyptian bondage, that in the promised land they might find rest, a rest memorialized in the weekly Sabbath (Deut. 5:14). The new event is the birth, life, death, resurrection, and ascension of Jesus; the interpretation of this new event, which takes up the old interpretation into itself in a reinterpretation, is that Jesus is the Christ, who gives his people rest from the bondage of sin, a final rest the Israelites could not obtain under Joshua when he brought them into Canaan.[28]

What is lacking in this otherwise helpful summary is reference to another Sabbath-oriented dialectic of "event interpretation" which Scripture suggests. In between the bookends of "Exodus" and "eschatology," there is the "event" of the Sabbath observance itself. Freed for the Sabbath by the events of the Exodus (i.e., by God's gracious acts of freedom on behalf of his people), the Israelites kept the Sabbath: they refrained from work. This led them to seek a theological interpretation of this further event—their Sabbath rest—and it was provided them in an analogy to the Creator himself (Gen. 2:1-3; Exod. 20:8-11).

2. The Advice of Qoheleth (Ecclesiastes)

Ecclesiastes would seem in many ways to be the least likely starting point for a biblical inroad to a theology of play. Although it is a wisdom book, its mood of resignation conveys a bleakness unique within the pages of Scripture:

Vanity of vanities, says the Preacher,
  vanity of vanities! All is vanity.
What does man gain by all the toil
  at which he toils under the sun?
. . . .
All things are full of weariness;
  a man cannot utter it;
the eye is not satisfied with seeing,
  nor the ear filled with hearing. (Eccl. 1:2-3, 8)

Qoheleth's intent in his book is to call into question our attempt to master life through our toil. He recognizes that the doctrine of retribution (so central to the wisdom tradition), in which the righteous are rewarded and the evil punished, does not always work out in practice. Not only do all of us share a common lot or destiny in death (Eccl. 2:15, 3:19, 5:13-17, 6:6, 7:2, 8:8, 9:2-3, 12:1-7), but all of us live an uncertain existence (Eccl. 4:13-16, 9:13-16) within an indiscernible moral order (Eccl. 3:16, 7:15, 8:14), where wisdom is easily defeated in the presence of riches or folly (Eccl. 9:17-10:1). Given all this, the arrogance of our effort to control or predict our fate is laughable. Wisdom's doctrine of retribution is naive—it does not match the facts of experience.

According to Qoheleth, our attempt to work at mastering life is misguided not only because life's experiences often frustrate the attempt (the "good guy" doesn't always win), but also because it constitutes an affront to the divine independence. We cannot presume to know God's will. God is sovereign and inscrutable (Eccl. 3:11; 6:10-11; 7:13-14, 23-24; 8:17). Thus, writes Qoheleth, we can neither find out what we are to do (Eccl. 6:12a, 7:29, 8:16-17) nor know what will come after us (Eccl. 6:12b, 9:11-15, 10:14, 11:4-6). Given life's experiences (which often undercut any notion of retribution) and God's inscrutability, all of our activities have merely the weight of one's breath (*hebel*). According to Qoheleth, they are like chasing after the wind (*rĕ'ût ruáḥ*; Eccl. 1:14).

How, then, in a book which James Crenshaw has labeled "pessimistic" and John Priest has called "cynical," do we look for a theology of play?[29] Would it not be easier to turn to Proverbs, where wisdom is said to have "played" (*saḥaq*) with God from before creation (Prov. 8:30), or perhaps to Psalm 104:26, where God is portrayed as playing with his creation? Perhaps the laughter of Abraham, which turned from cynical to celebratory when his son Isaac was born (the name means "He [God] laughs") would prove a more fruitful source for a biblical theology of play (Gen. 21). But such is not the case.

Even in this "extreme" book, which attempts to call into question our ability both to know God's will and to predict our fate, we find two root affirmations common to the wisdom tradition, based as it is in creation: (1) God is sovereign, and (2) present life is to be lived in joy as God's gift. Scholars of Ecclesiastes have often recognized the first of these tenets, but they have generally ignored or underplayed the latter. Gerhard Von Rad, for example, in his excellent book *Wisdom in Israel*, defines Qoheleth's "three basic insights round which his thoughts continually circle" as the following:

> 1. A thorough, rational examination of life is unable to find any satisfactory meaning: everything is "vanity." 2. God determines every event. 3. Man is unable to discern these decrees, the "works of God" in the world.[30]

Although this listing supports our above conclusions—that Qoheleth seeks to contradict the idea of retribution and to contradict the idea that we can know God's will—and although Von Rad recognizes, on the positive side, that Qoheleth affirms God's sovereignty, what is conspicuously ignored in his summary of Ecclesiastes is anything of the acceptance and enjoyment of life as a gift from God, which Qoheleth counsels.

There are, however, a few scholars who have recognized this more "playful" aspect of Qoheleth's teaching—that life is meant for our enjoyment. In his book *Koheleth—The Man and His World*, Robert Gordis discards his earlier focus on Qoheleth's alleged resignation and instead understands "the basic theme of the book" to be "*simhah*, the enjoyment of life."[31] Edwin Good concurs with Gordis, quoting him when he says:

> For Koheleth, joy is God's categorical imperative for man, not in any anemic or spiritualized sense, but rather as a full-blooded and tangible experience, expressing itself in the play of the body, and the activity of the mind, the contemplation of nature and the pleasures of love.[32]

And Norbert Lohfink expresses a similar viewpoint in the chapter "Man Face to Face With Death" in his book *The*

Christian Meaning of the Old Testament. Although Qoheleth's hatred of life has arisen from the stark fact of death, according to Lohfink, this is an intermediate stage. Qoheleth's final attitude, and the perspective from which he writes, is one of recognition of life's joys. We should accept "the gift of happiness in the present moment from the hand of God."[33]

Gordis, Good, and Lohfink all base their conclusions on a constant refrain found in Qoheleth which counterpoints the central emphasis of the wisdom writer's argument. Qoheleth asserts repeatedly that we are to enjoy life as God's gift (Eccl. 2:24-26, 3:12-13, 3:22; 5:18-20, 7:14, 8:15, 9:7-9, 11:9-12:1). This is our lot (*ḥēleq*), or portion, in life. Our active participation and engagement in the world is not to be manipulative or assertive but rather a seeing of (*rā'â*; Eccl. 2:24, 3:13, 5:18; cf. 9:9) or a rejoicing in (*sāmaḥ*; Eccl. 5:19; cf. 3:22, 8:15) the good in all our labor, an affirming as "good" (*tôb*) our eating and drinking (Eccl. 2:24-26, 5:18, 8:15, 9:7), a rejoicing in all our present activities (Eccl. 3:22), and an affirmation that life is meant to be lived joyfully in community (Eccl. 9:9, 4:9-12). Qoheleth preaches that we must accept life as given by God with both its joys and sorrows (Eccl. 7:14), and he argues for an active participation in and engagement with life, despite its uncertainties (Eccl. 11:1-6).

One can capture something of the flavor of Qoheleth's advice by quoting him:

> I know that there is nothing better for them [mankind] than to be happy and enjoy themselves as long as they live; also that it is God's gift to man that every one should eat and drink and take pleasure in all his toil. (Eccl. 3:12-13)

> Go, eat your bread with enjoyment, and drink your wine with a merry heart; for God has already approved what you do.
> Let your garments be always white; let not oil be lacking on your head.
> Enjoy life with the wife whom you love, all the days of your vain life which he has given you under the sun, because that is your portion in life and in your toil at which you toil under the sun. Whatever your hand finds to do, do it with your might; for there is no work or thought or knowledge or wisdom in Sheol, to which you are going. (Eccl. 9:7-10)

In the face of death, Qoheleth seeks to guide his readers into a joyful existence characterized by both work and play. Such joy is

not facile or simpleminded, but rather a recognition and celebration of created life:

> Light is sweet, and it is pleasant for the eyes to behold the
> sun.
> For if a man lives many years, let him rejoice in them all; but
> let him remember that the days of darkness will be many. (Eccl.
> 11:7-8)

Death becomes in Lohfink's phrase the "frontier situation" which
forces Qoheleth to reflect upon life.[34] Life is to be loved; its
present happiness and joy cherished. Such is the advice offered
by Qoheleth.

Gerhard Von Rad comments in passing that Qoheleth's concern in discussing God's determination of the "times" (*'et*) "is,
in the last resort, not a theoretical, or a theological one, but an
explicitly pastoral one."[35] In interpreting Ecclesiastes, scholars
have rightly pointed out the problems related to translating *Qoheleth* as "preacher." But despite the linguistic problems associated with this designation, it seems that the epithet "preacher,"
in the sense of "pastor," is indeed an appropriate one, at least
theologically.[36] According to Duncan Macdonald, we have done
Qoheleth an injustice by viewing his work as reflecting only a
spirit of resignation and despair. Qoheleth is not merely giving
his readers the pessimistic or cynical results of his attempt to
wrest meaning from life. Rather, he intends his book to be a
"guide to life."[37]

As a theological guide, the book of Ecclesiastes instructs
man (Qoheleth is writing to Hebrew young men) to take pleasure in his life. A man is to enjoy life with the woman he loves.
He is to eat and drink merrily. He is to dress festively. Moreover,
he is to enjoy his work as well, giving himself wholly to all that
he does. One's mistaken efforts at mastering life are doomed.
One must relax and enjoy life as it unfolds from God.

Are there any theological insights in Qoheleth's advice which
might prove helpful to us as we seek to delineate a theology of
play? How can we compare Qoheleth's instruction with our discussion of Sabbath play, for example? And how can his advice
serve as a helpful corrective to those theologians who embrace
the "Greek" and "Protestant" models of play?

Qoheleth is one with the Sabbath theologians who found
in the experience of play an impetus toward the divine. Play is
prefatory to our experience of God. George Hendry alludes to

this fact when he characterizes Qoheleth's preponderantly negative tone as used "only upon the misguided human endeavor to treat the created world as an end in itself." Hendry goes on to suggest that part of Qoheleth's purpose in writing as he does is to help people rediscover a God-centered joy. To accomplish this, Qoheleth must dispel our false and illusory hopes based upon our own toil. In this way he can assist us toward rediscovering our true happiness in God's gracious favor toward us (Eccl. 9:7).[38] Toward this end, Qoheleth exhorts his readers to play—to eat and drink with joy and to make love. For as we play, as we commune joyfully with creation and our fellow creatures, we become aware that life truly is a gift from God (Eccl. 2:24).

To the "Protestant," the Preacher affirms the value of play in and of itself. Our play need not serve our work. It has its own consequence, however unintended. Just as the Sabbath reminds us of our dependence upon divine grace, so, according to Qoheleth, our play experiences suggest God's gracious favor as their basis (Eccl. 2:24-26). Qoheleth wishes that he could find out what God has done from the beginning to the end (Eccl. 3:11), but God's special revelation eludes him. (This is one reason many Christian theologians have seen Qoheleth's writing as the final preparatory word of the Old Testament prior to God's breaking into history in the coming of Christ. The voice of salvation history had been silenced. A further word was needed from God.) But although Qoheleth cannot know God's saving ways, nevertheless he asserts from God's general revelation in his creation that our happiness and joy in our play is a gift from God. (Eccl. 2:24-26, 3:13, 5:19-20; cf. 3:22, 5:18, 9:9). Although God does not speak to Qoheleth in His role as Redeemer, His creation when experienced playfully points us to its source, God the Creator—the Giver of life.[39]

The book of Ecclesiastes also addresses those who would hold a "Greek" understanding of play. For although the Preacher calls us to play, such play is never apotheosized. We are not only to play but to find joy also in our labor (Eccl. 2:24, 3:13, 3:22, 5:18, 9:10; cf. 8:15, 9:9). Just as the Sabbath commandment states, "Six days you shall labor, and do all your work" (Exod. 20:9; Deut. 5:13), so too Qoheleth advises his readers to give themselves fully to their toil. But understood in the context of our joyful "play," this advice to work takes on a new perspective. Our toil is not meant to master life; it is not for the purpose of wresting the key to salvation from life itself. Rather, our work becomes in itself a creative, joyously free activity. When play becomes our teacher, work, like play, is discovered to have value, for it is part of life's gift that will one day end. We should work and play, suggests Qoheleth, but "playfully."[40]

Not only are we instructed to work playfully, but we are told we must play playfully. The biblical writer is clear on this point, for he portrays at length, by assuming the role of king, the vanity and emptiness of those "Greeks" who work at having fun (Eccl. 2:1-11). A life of unreserved play is but vanity: it is chasing after the wind. If the play world becomes one's all-consuming end, it ceases to be fulfilling. Qoheleth looks at life and observes people attempting to master it by playing. He holds up instead the vision of the "playful" person: one who is able to see (*rā'â*, "to indwell, look into, look at"; Eccl. 2:24, 3:13, 5:18; cf. 2:1, 5:19, 6:9) the good in life, rather than attempting to manipulate his surroundings. To "see" in this sense is to commune with and to enjoy the world as it is. Only in this way can one playfully work and play.

In *The Seduction of the Spirit,* Harvey Cox echoes something of the message of Ecclesiastes when he writes:

> To use a different metaphor, life for me is a two-step saraband of creating and letting be, of making and simply enjoying, of molding and then being molded, of work and play, prayer and politics, telling and listening. If you reduce it to a one-step, you might just as well stop the music, because it isn't really a dance any more.[41]

Qoheleth's model for a human life-style is clear: we are meant to be both people-for-others (workers) and people-with-others (players). Life is a two-step dance.

According to Karl Barth, Mozart recognized this fact. His life was characterized by both hard work and hard play (although he would have known what Cox does not—that you cannot two-step a saraband because it is in triple time). Barth, who loved Mozart's music and became something of an expert on it, described Mozart as possessing "unflinching industry," a man who worked a great deal during his "short life." And yet Mozart also loved to sit at the piano and improvise freely, sometimes for hours on end, without attempting later to write down what he had created. There was, according to Barth, "an entire Mozart world [his play world] which sounded once and then faded away for ever and ever!" Mozart laughed often, Barth says, although in a life plagued by money problems, illness, and professional disappointment, there was not much for him to laugh about. "Rather he laughed (and that is something absolutely different) because he was allowed and able to laugh in spite of all."[42] Here is that "Hebraic" model for play, one that challenges both our "Greek" and our "Protestant" conceptions by trustfully and joyously accepting a God-given rhythm for our work *and* for our play.

3. Love in the Song of Songs

The Bible concerns itself only rarely with the joyful play of human love. As Karl Barth observes, "The [erotic] notes are few."[43] Nevertheless, they are not absent, being centered (as one might suspect) in the creation-based discussion of Old Testament wisdom literature. For example, in Proverbs 5:15-19, we read:

> Drink water from your own cistern,
>   flowing water from your own well.
> Should your springs be scattered abroad,
>   streams of water in the streets?
> Let them be for yourself alone,
>   and not for strangers with you.
> Let your fountain be blessed,
>   and rejoice in the wife of your youth,
>   a lovely hind, a graceful doe.
> Let her affection fill you at all times with delight,
>   be infatuated always with her love.

The writer here goes beyond merely prohibiting adultery. Love is viewed as a refreshing fountain, the beloved as a "creature" both lovely and to be loved. Affection and infatuation are to characterize the envisioned relationship. It should be delightful.

Such advice has its theological beginning in the second chapter of Genesis, where the woman is described as being created, for God saw that it was "not good that the man should be alone" (Gen. 2:18). In relating the story, the writer of Genesis records the man's exclamation upon seeing his mate:

> "This at last is bone of my bones
>   and flesh of my flesh;
> she shall be called Woman [Heb. *ishshah*]
>   because she was taken out of Man [Heb. *ish*]." (Gen. 2:23)

The partnership of husband and wife is understood by this writer as "life's chief blessing."[44] Love is not deified, as it typically was by Israel's neighbors. It is not even personified. Instead, as Jean Paul Audet points out, it is portrayed simply "as a good which man and woman [hold] from God by their common origin."[45]

The goodness of love as created by God is taken up again by the prophet Hosea, who uses the continuing infatuation and affection he has for his wife, Gomer, as an image of the love Yahweh has for his people Israel. It is not the fruitfulness of marriage that he draws upon, not the possibility of procreation, but, in Audet's words, "an aspect which is in a sense much more radical, and which is more specifically human, namely that of love."[46] Hosea's complaint about his marriage has nothing to do with sterility or lack of progeny. In fact, Gomer has borne him two sons and a daughter (Hos. 1:39). Hosea is torn apart by something else—Gomer's unfaithfulness. Nevertheless, his love for her is unquenchable, and he sets out to woo Gomer back. He creates a new affection for her. Hosea's point is that God's plan for his wayward people is rooted in a love analogous to that of a man for a woman.

But it is not to Proverbs or Hosea—not even to Genesis 1 and 2—that one must turn to see the full expanse of human love portrayed. It is the Song of Songs that provides the fullest commentary. Barth calls it the "Magna Carta" of humanity.[47] In it the implications of the creation accounts of the love of a man for a woman are put into song. If the song were not in the Bible, the playfulness of its uninhibited yet delicate descriptions would be clear to all. But because the Song is in the Scriptures, it has most often been moralized or spiritualized, being understood as an allegory of the love God has for his people. Perhaps Saint Jerome can be seen as typical in this regard, offering the following advice to Laeta about her daughter: "Let her never look upon her own nakedness. She should not read the Song of Songs until she has read Chronicles and Kings, for otherwise she might not observe that the book refers only to spiritual love."[48]

When an allegorical interpretation of the Song first developed is debated. The Mishnah quotes Rabbi Akiba at the council of Jammia in 90 A.D. as saying, "For all the writings are holy, but the Song of Songs is the Holy of Holies."[49] The same rabbi is reputed to have said later: "Anyone who, for the sake of entertainment, sings the Song as though it were a profane song, will have no share in the World to Come."[50] From evidence such as this, it seems safe to conclude that the allegorical interpretation of the Song arose in reaction to those who were suggesting its largely secular character. As Calvin Seerveld notes, ". . . allegorical exegesis of The Greatest Song originated as a defense against the complaint, 'How can such worldly love poetry be holy and a norm for the faith?' Allegorizing of the Song was a theological construction formed to answer critics sceptical of the Song's canonical status already assumed."[51]

The allegorizing of the Song's wonder concerning human love was given impetus by the early Christian scholar Origen, who contended that all language had a literal, a figurative, and a spiritual, or allegorical, sense. Such an approach, for example, led Cyril of Alexandria to interpret chapter one, verse thirteen ("My beloved is to me a bag of myrrh, that lies between my breasts") as referring to the Old and New Testaments, between which hangs Christ.[52] Not all interpretation that followed through the centuries was as ludicrous as this, although much of it was. As Seerveld points out, "Generation after generation of Christian scholars kept reading past the obvious sense of what was before them and spent their sanctified ingenuity ascertaining the hidden 'spiritual' meaning of the words, so as to lead the inexperienced laity into the way of mystical truth."[53] Saint Bernard of Clairvaux, for example, preached eighty-six lengthy sermons on the first two chapters of the Song, and found its single focus to be Christ's love for his Church.

Not all accepted such spiritualizing, but the cost of opposition ran high. Theodore of Mopsuestia (360-427 A.D.) was anathematized; Sebastian Castellio was deported from Geneva by Calvin; and Luis de Leon fell under the Inquisition. It was not until the Enlightenment that the vitality and passion of this love song could be recognized freely (the poet Johann Gottfried von Herder was one of the first to find its theme to be human love). But even then its "literal" advocates were few. Only in the twentieth century has biblical scholarship advanced to the place where the Song's "sheer, ecstatic enjoyment of human love between a man and a woman" (Seerveld) can be recognized.[54] In his highly influential essay "The Interpretation of the Song of Songs," H. H. Rowley speaks for most modern commentators when he concludes, "The view I adopt finds in it nothing but what it appears to be, lovers' songs, expressing their delight in one another and the warm emotions of their hearts. All of the other views find in the Song what they bring to it."[55]

A second issue of interpretation besides the tradition of allegorization must be faced by the reader of the Song. This has to do with its traditional status as a wisdom book. In its canonical form, the Song of Songs is a collection of songs (some going back to the Solomonic era and all being brought together in honor of Solomon), most likely edited by Israel's wisdom teachers in the post-exilic period. The question is, Was the book meant *to instruct* us concerning the nature of love? E. J. Young believes this is the case, arguing strongly for the Song's didactic intent:

> The Song does celebrate the dignity and purity of human love. This is a fact which has not always been sufficiently stressed. The Song, therefore, is didactic and moral in its purpose. It comes to us in this world of sin, where lust and passion are on every hand, where fierce temptations assail us and try to turn us aside from the God-given standard of marriage. And it reminds us, in particularly beautiful fashion, how pure and noble true love is.[56]

On the other hand, W. J. Fuerst writes: "It is fruitless to try to establish that this book teaches us about theology, or God's love, or even man's love. The book was written to celebrate, not to teach."[57] The issue might be defined as follows: Is the book a song or a lesson? If it is a lesson, then a certain somberness of tone is easily construed. If it is a song, then a lighter, more joyous spirit seems truer to its original intention.

One can complicate the issue quite easily. That the Song is a collection of songs implies a pre-history, a pre-literary period, for the individual pieces. It suggests that there might have been a variety of life settings for parts of the Song (courtship, wedding, etc.). It also suggests a possible distancing of the original vibrancy and playfulness of the songs; they became a kind of lesson. But our knowledge of this pre-literary period is totally inferential.[58] And even if the Song is now meant to instruct us, and even if we are ignorant of the exact number of original poems and of their context, it seems safe to conclude with Jean Paul Audet that the text remains first of all a song and not a lesson.[59] This conclusion implies an intended "state of consciousness" distinct from the earnestness that so easily befalls instruction—even instruction about the playfulness of love between a man and a woman. We must not ignore the book's edited title. This collection of songs has a basic unity. It is to be received as a song—in fact, as the greatest of songs, for that is what the phrase "Song of Songs" means in the Hebrew.

M. H. Segal is correct in observing that the text's joyous, youthful spirit as a song has seldom been recognized. "Its happy optimism, its gaiety, its love of good-natured fun" has been overlooked by most of its commentators, he says: "They have invested the Song with a serious edifying character which does not fit it at all. It abounds in playfulness, in gentle raillery and fun, mingled with touching sentiments of love and tenderness."[60] Segal hypothesizes that the original setting for the songs was the Solomonic era, when the horses of Pharaoh's chariots would have walked the streets of Jerusalem (S. of S. 1:5; cf. 1 Kgs. 3:1), when the details of life from Damascus to En Gedi would have been known (S. of S. 6:5, 4:8, 1:14, 4:1, 7:5-6; cf. 1 Kgs. 5:1-4), and when life had a certain luxurious quality (S. of S. 1:10; cf. Isa. 3:23). According to Segal, "The whole tone of the Song" with "its delight in love and in good living and in pleasant things" best suits "the reign of Solomon . . . when 'Judah and Israel were many . . . eating and drinking and making merry' (1 Kings IV 20)."[61]

Segal's point is somewhat overdrawn, but it is a healthy corrective to much interpretation of the Song. Whether his assessment of the pre-literary history of these songs is correct or not, there is no doubt that the songs are the poetry of lovers. They contain nothing artificial. The varied aspects of human love-play are everywhere in view. Perhaps the clearest evidence of love's playfulness in the Song is the strong feminine presence within the work. The product of a patriarchal society, the Song's perspective is nonetheless egalitarian. In fact, it might be argued that a "new set of rules" has been adopted so that the emphasis falls on the female. Hyam Maccoby notes, for example, the "immodest behavior of the female lover" and calls this "the main enigma" of the song.[62] It is the woman who most often sets out to "capture" the man. From the beginning, the female's sexual desire is uninhibitedly expressed: "O that you would kiss me"; "Draw me after you"; "Awake, O north wind"; "Let my beloved come to his garden, and eat its choicest fruits"; "Come, my beloved, let us go forth into the fields" (S. of S. 1:2, 1:4, 4:16, 7:11). Here is female sexuality openly expressed, sensual yet tasteful. None of the strictures of the larger male-dominated culture is apparent. Judaism often gloried in the achievements of its patriarchalism, but here another perspective dominates. After all, "All's fair in love and. . . ."

That the interaction of the lovers in the Song is indeed play is seen in the brief dialogue that opens chapter two. There the woman describes herself as just one flower among many. Perhaps she is being a little coquettish. The man responds playfully by saying, "As a lily among brambles, so is my love among maidens" (S. of S. 2:2). To this the woman responds, returning the compliment, "As an apple tree among the trees of the wood, so is my beloved among young men" (S. of S. 2:3). The song of mutual admiration ends as the woman reflects on her time apart (her "playtime") with her beloved: "With great delight I sat in his shadow, and his fruit was sweet to my taste" (S. of S. 2:3).

That the Song of Songs is to be interpreted in the context of the joyful play of lovers is also suggested by the opening song (S. of S. 1:2-4), a poem which, as Jean Paul Audet says, has "no close textual connection with what follows."[63] If one were not interested in establishing a playful mood of ecstasy and joy, it would seem more logical to begin the song with verse five, where the woman introduces herself to the daughters of Jerusalem. The author, however, wants us to experience something of the emotion of love. He is not presenting an academic discussion. Thus he has the woman express her desire to be kissed. In reflecting on these opening verses, Audet has even suggested that the author chose to begin the collection with this song in order to provide a suitable title for the text: "O that you would kiss me. . . ." According to this hypothesis, the appreciative superscription in verse one would be understood as coming from the pen of a later editor, from someone who recognized the merit of the Song and had deep affection for it. Audet asks, Is it likely that an author would call his own song "the most beautiful of songs"?

Throughout the Song the lovers take mutual delight in each other's physical and spiritual charms. Although the language is never crude or clinical, its explicitness takes it beyond the normal discourse of the workaday world. The enthusiastic praise of the physical beauties of the man and the woman seems more appropriate to descriptions of lovers, or to their conversations, or perhaps to the songs of a wedding ceremony. It is impossible to pin down the particular life settings for these songs; no doubt they are various. But the general context, surely, is the love play of ancient Israel. As we listen to the Song, we overhear the lovers teasing one another (e.g., S. of S. 2:14-15) or dreaming (e.g., S. of S. 3:1-5). We observe the wedding procession (S. of S. 3:6-11) and hear the beauty of the beloved described (e.g., S. of S. 4:1-7). We read of the erotic pleasures which the lover finds in his beloved (S. of S. 6:2-3). There is a description of a surprise rendezvous between the lover and the beloved in a garden (S. of S. 6:11-12). There is even a portrayal (a *wasf*) of the woman's physical beauty as she dances, a description that begins with her graceful feet and ascends slowly and graphically upward to her head (S. of S. 6:13-7:5). We overhear a dialogue about sexual desire (S. of S. 7:6-10), which is followed by another song in which the woman declares her willingness to give herself sexually to her lover (S. of S. 7:11-13). The Song ends with what M. A. van den Oudenrijn has suggested might derive from a game of "hide and seek" played by two people in love.[64] To the biblical writer the value of such love play is immeasurable. Although love's extravagances might seem irrelevant to life's larger concerns, they are in reality fundamental. He summarizes:

> . . . love is strong as death. . . .
> Its flashes are flashes of fire,
>   a most vehement flame. . . .
> If a man offered for love
>   all the wealth of his house,
>   it would be utterly scorned. (S. of S. 8:6-7)

Such is the nature of the Song of Songs—a beautiful, extended paean to human love. We would be untrue to the text if we ended our discussion here, however. Two comments of wider import are necessary. First, in his helpful article entitled "Sensuous Theology," David Fraser notes that the Book of Proverbs provides a number of counterpoints to the Song:

> The same erotic language employed by the lovers in the Song without negative connotation is condemned when found on the harlot's lips (Prov. 5:3, 6:25, 7:15, 17, 18; Song 3:1, 4:6, 9, 5:5,

8:1). Sexual love may exist for its own sake in the Song, but . . . Proverbs relativizes human love by placing it within the established order of life and questions of prudence. The Song is not concerned as such with whether the lovers are foolish or wise, or whether love must be evaluated by major ethical norms.[65]

That is, like play more generally, sexual love can be "bastardized."[66] What might have all the appearances of love play might in fact be nothing of the sort. It can prove inauthentic and manipulative, as the writer of Proverbs is quick to caution. But such larger ethical considerations are beyond the purview of the writer of the Song. His focus is on the simple wonder of love.

Secondly, although the Song has no allegorical intention, the community of faith, both Jewish and Christian, was in one sense correct in seeking to find analogies between the sexual love described in the Song of Songs and the supernatural love God has for his people. According to Donald Bloesch, it is not inappropriate to see a "reflection of God's love for his people and of the human response to this love" in the sexual love between a man and a woman.[67] This prophetic theme is repeatedly mentioned in the pages of Scripture and is the central image of the Book of Hosea, as we have already observed. Roland Murphy notes, "How remarkable that Israel could understand the Lord as beyond sex, and thus proscribe fertility cult, and yet could exalt him as spouse."[68]

One must recognize, however, that in moving beyond the intention of the Song, in moving from creation theology to covenantal theology, in speaking of God's love for his people, one is assuming a prior and definitive understanding of God. That is, general revelation is congruent with special revelation, but one cannot derive the covenant from creation. This was the mistake we observed in Sam Keen's thinking. His natural theology based in the person at play necessarily had to remain "agnostic." Donald Bloesch warns, "Beginning with human love and then trying to find in it the key that opens the doorway to divine love only ends in a false mysticism."[69] There is in human sexuality a sense of awe, intuition, and ecstasy that brings with it a "suspicion of holiness." Love's playground can, indeed, be a "consecrated spot." Human sexuality can, in Bonhoeffer's words, "keep a ground-base of joy alive" in all of us, and in this way prepare us for, and help sustain us within, our ongoing life of faith. But it cannot clarify the central wonder of God's grace.

4. Israel at "Play"

The descriptions of the "play" of the Sabbath and of the play of lovers, like the advice to play found in Ecclesiastes, find their theological center in God the Creator. But biblical discussions of play are not limited to these creational perspectives. If one reads the biblical record carefully, one will observe the importance of play even within the more dominant biblical discussion of God's saving activity on behalf of his people. In particular, Israel's God-intended play is evident in descriptions of her festivals and of her love for dance. It is basic to the importance attached to feasting. It is even central to her practice of hospitality.

Many of the texts having to do with such play have intentions other than to instruct us about play. That is why we have begun this biblical overview with the creation-centered texts on play. But a description of Israel's life-style is nonetheless instructive, for it models in a culturally specific way a more general pattern that views play as an important component of life. Even if the customs of hospitality might change, or even if such rites of passage as weaning might no longer be celebrated, the larger issue — the importance of play — remains evident.

A. Festival   Religious festivals were occasions for a break from life's larger concerns, a special time, or "parenthesis" within life, consecrated to the Lord in joy. We read in Nehemiah, for example, that the Israelites gathered to hear Ezra read the Book of the Law of Moses. After he had read clearly from the Law and the Levites had helped instruct the people in it, Nehemiah, together with Ezra and the Levites, had to correct the people for failing to celebrate their God:

> "This day is holy to the Lord your God; do not mourn or weep."
> For all the people wept when they heard the words of the law.
> Then he said to them, "Go your way, eat the fat and drink sweet
> wine and send portions to him for whom nothing is prepared; for
> this day is holy to our Lord; and do not be grieved, for the joy of
> the Lord is your strength." So the Levites stilled all the people,

saying, "Be quiet, for this day is holy; do not be grieved." And all the people went their way to eat and drink and to send portions and to make great rejoicing, because they had understood the words that were declared to them. (Neh. 8:9-12)

Nehemiah's call to festivity assumes that holiness is better associated with joy than solemnity, with happiness rather than gloom. He would have the people eat rich food ("the fat") and drink sweet wine. Moreover, to insure that everyone can participate in the celebration (and thus, perhaps, to make sure that larger ethical questions do not intrude and abort the time of play), he counsels that food and drink should even be sent to those who would otherwise be left out. The festival is for all.

The description of this holiday (holy-day) is followed in the Book of Nehemiah by the discovery that God had intended this festival to last seven days and to include the building of booths for the people to live in temporarily while they celebrated. The booths were a reminder of the Exodus, when the Israelites camped along the way. These structures were to be made from the "branches of olive, wild olive, myrtle, palm and other leafy trees" (Neh. 8:15). This Feast of Booths, or Feast of Tabernacles, as it came to be called, took place at harvest-time. "But notice what it did," J. Webb Mealy says: "it drew man's interest away from gloating over his *accomplishments* [in the successful harvest] back to rejoicing in who he *was* by virtue of God's election and love. Everyone had to live in booths made of pretty branches . . . enjoyable but not so because of human ingenuity."[70] That is, the festival with its new "playground" (the booths) and "playtime" (seven days during the seventh month) became an occasion to rejoice in who God was and in what he had done for his people.

The story of Esther provides another example of the playfulness of Jewish festivals, giving a rationale for the feast of Purim (Esth. 9:26). Although the enemy had cast their lot (Heb. *Pur*) to destroy the Jews, with the help of Esther and Mordecai, the *Pur* fell on the wicked. The Jews thus were able to celebrate with "a day for gladness and feasting and holiday-making, and a day on which they send choice portions to one another" (Esth. 9:19). As a result, the celebration is said to have become a yearly event, when "mourning" is turned to "holiday" as "feasting and gladness" prevail (Esth. 9:22). As with the Feast of Booths,

Purim was based, at least implicitly, in the activity of God on behalf of his people. As such it was meant to qualify one's work at mastering life.

In Deuteronomy 16, when Moses addresses the people of Israel gathered before him on the plains of Moab, he describes the three major festivals in Israel's early life: the Feast of the Passover and Unleavened Bread (vv. 1-8); the Feast of Weeks, or "Pentecost" (vv. 9-12); and the Feast of Booths (vv. 13-15). In the descriptions the feasts are patterned on a sabbatical scheme, reinforcing the idea that they are to be a time of rest, not work. Nothing specifically playful is mentioned in connection with the first of these, the Festival of the Passover. It was, however, to be a week in which no work was done (v. 8), and in which the animals sacrificed each evening were to be eaten completely. On the other hand, both the Festival of Weeks and the Festival of Booths were to be characterized by rejoicing (vv. 9, 14; cf. Lev. 23:40). As with the Passover, these other holy days were holidays on which the people made a pilgrimage to Yahweh's sanctuary (v. 16). There, with all of the community gathered together, Israel celebrated the goodness of the Lord in providing food. They were, said Moses, to "indeed be joyful" (v. 15).

B. *Dance*   The Old Testament makes repeated references to dance, suggesting that it served an important function in ancient Jewish culture. In the Book of Job, for example, Job complains that he is suffering while the wicked prosper. In describing their well-being, he laments that not only do their bulls breed but "their children dance. They sing to the tambourine and the lyre, and rejoice to the sound of the pipe" (Job 21:11-12). Job is in no way critical of such playful dance. He only complains that the wrong parties are participating. It is his family that should be dancing, not mourning (cf. Luke 15:25). As if seeking to answer Job's complaint, the writer of Ecclesiastes reflects: "For everything there is a season . . . a time to mourn, and a time to dance" (Eccl. 3:1-4). Similarly, in Lamentations Jeremiah bemoans the destruction of Jerusalem, saying: "The joy of our hearts has ceased; our dancing has been turned to mourning" (Lam. 5:15; cf. Ps. 30:11, Jer. 31:13).

On a more positive note, the Psalmist advises his listeners

to praise the Lord "with dancing" (Ps. 149:3; cf. Ps. 87:7, 150:4). And the Israelites often did just that, as when they danced in celebration after David had repulsed the Philistines. We read: "As they were coming home . . . the women came out of all the cities of Israel, singing and dancing, to meet King Saul, with timbrels, with songs of joy, and with instruments of music. And the women sang to one another as they made merry, 'Saul has slain his thousands, and David his ten thousands' " (1 Sam. 18:6-7; cf. Judg. 11:34, Exod. 15:20, 21). Dance seems to have been a common feature of life in ancient Israel, particularly at festival time. In fact, the very words for festival in the Hebrew seem to originate as terms for dancing.[71] Judges 21 describes the dance of the daughters of Shiloh, most probably during an autumn harvest festival. Similarly, Psalm 68 portrays a processional dance up to Zion, accompanied by singers and timbrel players (cf. Ps. 118:27). And Jeremiah looks foward to the time after the exile when Israel will once again be able to celebrate at their festivals, when they will "go forth in the dance of the merrymakers" (Jer. 31:4).[72]

Perhaps the most vivid recounting of Israel's playful dancing is the account of David when he brought the "ark of God" (the Ark of the Covenant) to Zion. While thirty thousand men of Israel paraded, it says, "David and all the house of Israel were making merry before the Lord with all their might, with songs and lyres and harps and tambourines and castanets and cymbals" (2 Sam. 6:5). A tragedy brought the celebration to a halt, and the ark was temporarily stored in the house of Obed-edom; but David later retrieved it and brought the ark "to the city of David with rejoicing. . . . And David danced before the Lord with all his might; and David was girded with a linen ephod. So David and all the house of Israel brought up the ark of the Lord with shouting, and with the sound of the horn" (2 Sam. 6:12, 14-15). The narrative continues, relating how Michal, David's wife, was angry at him for leaping and dancing before the Lord, uncovering himself "as one of the vulgar fellows shamelessly uncovers himself" (2 Sam. 6:20). But David rebuked her, saying, "I will make merry before the Lord" (2 Sam. 6:21). And the account ends with the editorial comment about God's judgment on the matter: "And Michal the daugher of Saul had no child to the day of her death" (2 Sam. 6:23).

The above text is instructive because it describes the worshipful, yet playful, way Israel celebrated her good fortune. It involved, for example, the use of a wide variety of musical instruments. Moreover, even David could adopt a new set of "rules" during this "playtime," wearing only an ephod for his dance. When Michal objected that he would be thought "one of the vulgar fellows," i.e., that such action wasn't proper for a king, David responded that the maids (the commoners) would not object but would revere him for his merriment before the Lord. Michal could not let David "play"; matters of propriety and station intruded. (It is interesting to observe that such revelry must not have been uncommon among the larger citizenry, because Michal compared David's informality with what a common person might do.) But David would not distance himself from his people during the celebration. There was a bond among the celebrants that made his simple attire appropriate.

David's dance before the ark can be contrasted with the licentious dancing of the Israelites before the golden calf in Moses' day. Wanting to be like their Baal-worshiping neighbors, the Israelites succumbed to orgiastic dancing (Exod. 32:19). The text states that "the people sat down to eat and drink, and rose up to play" (Exod. 32:6). The verb "play" in Hebrew is the same word that is translated "fondle" in Genesis 26:8. It has a clear sexual reference. The description of Israel's play in front of the calf suggests a drunken orgy that included dance. In the years to come Israel would repeatedly be tempted to direct her celebratory dancing to Baal, not Yahweh (cf. the account of Jeroboam in 1 Kings 12 and the repeated reference to the sins of Jeroboam throughout the book). But in this context the relevant point is not the temptation to idolatry; it is the constancy of Israel's "play." The Israelites danced before their God — whether in their faith that god was Yahweh, or in their unbelief, Baal.

C. Feasting   Special moments in the Israelites' lives often included a feast, a meal that went beyond mere physical maintenance and became an act of play. When Sarah weaned Isaac, for example, "Abraham made a great feast" (Gen. 21:8). But on that occasion Sarah refused to enter into the "playtime," seeing Ishmael, who was "playing with her son Isaac," as a potential threat to Isaac's inheritance. That is, matters from the larger arena of life intruded and dampened the feast's intended joy. In Genesis 29, a similar feast is described, this time to celebrate Jacob's marriage. Again, the feast has a surprising and sobering ending, as Jacob discovers the next morning that his wife is not Rachel, his intended bride, but Leah, her older sister. Nevertheless, something of Israel's style of playful feasting is evident. (One recalls here the wedding feast at Cana, when Jesus assured its success by turning water into wine. Cf. John 2.)

It is this Jewish custom of celebrating important moments in one's life with a feast that Jesus uses in his parable of the prodigal son. After the father's younger son took his inheritance and squandered "his property in loose living," he returned home filled with remorse, expecting to be punished. But the father responded in love, telling his servants, " 'Bring quickly the best robe, and put it on him; and put a ring on his hand, and shoes on his feet; and bring the fatted calf and kill it, and let us eat and make merry. . . .' And they began to make merry" (Luke 15:22-24).

When the older brother returned, however, he was angered by the feast in progress. He resented having his wayward brother honored in this way. The father responded, " 'It was fitting to make merry and be glad, for this your brother was dead, and is alive; he was lost, and is found' " (Luke 15:32). As with the occasions of weaning and marriage, this was a time for joyful feasting.

Jesus tells this parable to instruct us about the nature of God himself. But it is important to note the context Luke provides for it (Luke 15:1-3). Jesus is responding to criticism that he, like the father in the story, is "feasting" with the wrong people. One recalls here the earlier words of rebuke directed at Jesus, when he is criticized for his "eating and drinking": " 'Behold, a glutton and a drunkard, a friend of tax collectors and sinners!' " (Luke 7:34; cf. Luke 5:29, 14:13). Jesus' life-style seems to have included sufficient feasting with "sinners" and other "undesirables" that it scandalized the religious establishment. The scandal, one should note, was not his feasting as such; this was part of Israel's customary activity. The offense was Jesus' choice of co-celebrants. Like Michal in her disapproval of David, the Pharisees could not allow Jesus to join with the "vulgar."

The association of feasts with significant moments in life finds its ultimate use as an eschatological symbol of celebration and renewal. Although Israel will be judged for her apostasy, God will restore her one day. Isaiah portrays that future hope, saying, "On this mountain the Lord of hosts will make for all peoples a feast of fat things, a feast of wine on the lees, of fat things full of marrow, of wine on the lees well refined" (Isa. 25:6). Zechariah speaks similarly of future "cheerful feasts" (Zech. 8:18). Our feasting, like the rest of the Sabbath and the play of lovers, becomes symbolic of God's gracious presence with us. Thus in the book of Revelation John portrays a marriage feast which is to last throughout eternity: " 'Blessed are those who are invited to the marriage supper of the Lamb' " (Rev. 19:9). The Christian's feast will one day know no end.

D. Hospitality   Caring for the stranger (sojourner) was a sacred duty for the Israelite. With public inns rare and the threat of robbery real, hospitality was a necessary and reciprocal service. In fact, its provision was so important that its disregard was considered a sin deserving the severest penalty. (Note, for example, that the chief sin of Sodom, according to the prophet Ezekiel, was inhospitality, not sexual perversion; cf. Ezek. 16:49.)

The book of Judges records the inhospitable treatment given a certain Levite by the Benjaminites of Gibeah. As was the custom, this Levite entered the city and sat down in the open square. But no one took him and his party in to spend the night (Judg. 19:15). Finally, an old man from the hill country of Ephraim offered him provisions, fearing for the wayfarer's safety. As the men were "making their hearts merry" with food and drink, others from the city came and demanded that the old man give up his guest so that they might homosexually attack him. Resisting unsuccessfully, the man and his guest were able to escape this violation only by letting the men of the city repeatedly rape the guest's concubine instead. After a night of abuse, the woman was found dead on the host's doorstep. The Levite left town only to rally the Israelites to war against these evildoers. And even after the Benjaminites proved dangerous adversaries, fell-ing twenty-two thousand Israelites, the Israelites persisted, for such an offense must not go unpunished.

The evilness of the people of Benjamin was evident in their gross inhospitality. The guest deserved respect and protection, even if he were an enemy, up to three days after eating with the host. There were few more basic ordinances in ancient life (cf. Gen. 24:22ff., Exod. 2:20, Deut. 23:4, Judg. 13:15, 1 Sam. 25, 2 Sam. 12:1-6, 1 Kgs. 17:8-16, Neh. 5:17-19, Job 22:7, 31:32).

The ethical force of the obligation to be hospitable was formidable in ancient Israel. But being gracious to one's guests had another side as well. Not only were the guest and his party to be *cared for,* they were to be *entertained.* Hospitality was not only a *duty*; it was meant to be a *delight.* In the account from Judges 19 just described, the text says that the old man from Ephraim made his guests' "hearts merry" (v. 22).

An even better example of hospitality's "playful" intent is found earlier in the same chapter. Judges 19 tells the story of this same Levite traveling in the remote hill country of Ephraim after his concubine had become angry and had gone to her parents' home. After several months the Levite came to her, speaking kindly, and tried to bring her back. On seeing him, the woman's father welcomed the Levite warmly and "made him stay, and he remained with him three days; so they ate and drank, and lodged there" (Judg. 19:4). This was the accepted practice of the time — offering the sojourner three days of hospitality.

But the woman's father wanted to do even more for his guest, so he continued to offer him food. "So the two men sat and ate and drank together; and the woman's father said to the man, 'Be pleased [again] to spend the night, and let your heart be merry' " (Judg. 19:6). And the Levite did. On the fifth day the father pleaded once again with his son-in-law to tarry and to make his heart merry. It was only toward evening that the son-in-law, with his concubine and servant, was able to break away. While his guest was present, the father put aside other concerns, eating and drinking with him. His goal was to make his guest happy.

Perhaps the clearest Old Testament example of the cultural importance of hospitality as an occasion for "play" is the description in Genesis 18 and 19 of the visits to Abraham and Lot by the divine messengers, who offered them salvation from the impending judgment on Sodom. Claus Westermann, in his helpful essay "Work, Civilization and Culture in the Bible," comments:

> If we read this story carefully and take in its finer points, we realize that the visit of the three men is presented as a cultural event. A visit of this kind was a red-letter day for the nomadic people of that region and period. It stood out from the long days and weeks when they saw no one. Because it was so special, a meeting of this kind became a festive event, where every gesture, every word and every act had form and style. With exquisite respect and "courtesy" (though there were no courts as yet) the guests were greeted, invited in, welcomed and given food and drink. In this framework the words that were exchanged took on great importance. It was not a question of "conversation" in the trivial sense. . . . Words exchanged during a visit of this kind were cherished and passed on.[73]

It is important to realize that neither Abraham nor Lot knew of the secret identity of their heavenly visitors when they opened their houses to them. Both, however, went to greet these total strangers, bowing to the ground according to the custom. As the gracious host, Abraham tried to minimize his involvement. He asked if he could provide a "morsel of bread" and "a little water." In actuality, he ordered a feast, and conversation developed naturally. Only the best flour was used—abundantly—to make the bread. Milk and a form of yogurt were served, as was meat from a choice calf which was slaughtered for the occasion. The strong custom of hospitality was reinforced by Lot's actions the next day. After leaving Abraham, the visitors traveled to Sodom; there Lot, who is otherwise portrayed in Genesis as a self-interested person (cf. Gen. 13), rose to greet them. And unwilling to take "no" for an answer, he took the guests to his home, where there was water for bathing their feet, food for their hungry stomachs, and safety from attack.

A final example of Old Testament hospitality is found in Psalm 23. In his time of crisis the Psalmist sings a song of trust to his Lord. He thinks back to his youth and finds effective analogies for his God's actions in his shepherding experiences and in the Near Eastern customs of hospitality practiced by his family. Wanting not to argue the truth but to sing it, he seeks to fill his listeners' minds with the wonder and glory of God.

God is that good shepherd who provides, leads, and protects. He is also a gracious host offering abundant hospitality:

> Thou preparest a table before me
> in the presence of my enemies;
> thou anointest my head with oil,
> my cup overflows. (Ps. 23:5)

Like Lot (Gen. 19), God will not let the threat of attack stop him from preparing a lavish table. Beyond offering us protection, God as host will be our gracious supplier. He will freshen the hair and faces of his guests with olive oil after their travel. He will serve them a cup so full of refreshment that it literally overflows. God will meet his people's needs personally and abundantly. With such a playful prospect, the Psalmist can predict surely that goodness and mercy will follow him, for he is God's guest. Moreover, he will dwell in God's house, not just for three days but for ever.[74]

5. The Friendship of Jesus

One will look in vain for a fully developed theology of play in the New Testament. Paul refers to athletic competition as he describes the Christian's life (1 Cor. 9:24-27, Phil. 3:13-14, 2 Tim. 4:7), but his point is not about sports. We have already mentioned Jesus' parable of the prodigal son and have alluded to his participation in the wedding feast at Cana. Feasts seem to have been a frequent experience for Jesus; he often used them symbolically in his teaching (cf. Matt. 9:14-17, 22:1-14, 25:1-13). By and large, however, there is little formal mention in Scripture of the play of Jesus or of the early church — and for good reason. The New Testament focuses on the Gospel, the "good news" about Jesus Christ. The text is so centered on this news that everything else is relegated to secondary status. Moreover, the events of the New Testament took place during a relatively short period of time, and during these years the *mission* of the Church captured the necessary attention of the early Christians. Paul, for example, in light of the importance of the evangelistic task, wished that Christians would even postpone marriage (cf. 1 Cor. 7:1, 7, 26, 32f.).

Some have found even this absence of reflection on play evocative. G. K. Chesterton, for example, concludes his autobiographical reflections with these words:

> And as I close this chaotic volume I open again the strange small book from which all Christianity came; and I am again haunted by a kind of confirmation. The tremendous figure which fills the Gospels towers in this respect, as in every other, above all the thinkers who ever thought themselves tall. His pathos was natural, almost casual. . . . He never restrained His anger. . . . Yet He restrained something. . . . There was some one thing that was too great for God to show us when He walked upon our earth; and I have sometimes fancied that it was His mirth.[75]

More appropriate, surely, is the comment of Gary Warner in his book on a Christian approach to competition:

> If one wishes to point a finger at God for leaving anything out of the New Testament, it could be in the area of play. The Gospels are a pretty serious proposition. While books have been written about the humorous Jesus and the playful Jesus, this requires an abundance of speculation, conjecture, and deductive reasoning as well as more than a pinch of wishful thinking.[76]

There is, however, one aspect of the New Testament record which has received scant attention and which might qualify as authentic play: Jesus' friendships, which were clearly important to him. In Luke 7, for example, Jesus contrasts his convivial life-style with John the Baptist's ascetic approach. John's life was a living parable of the need to repent, but his critics rejected it as demon-possessed. Jesus' style, on the other hand, embodied the future kingdom of joy. While John withdrew, Jesus enjoyed the company of others so much that his critics scolded: " 'Behold, a glutton and a drunkard, a friend of tax collectors and sinners!' " (Luke 7:34).

That Jesus was truly a friend of those often judged undesirable is reinforced by Luke, who follows the above account with a description of a dinner Jesus attended at the house of a Pharisee. While he was sitting at the table, "a woman of the city, who was a sinner" (most probably a prostitute or an adulteress), entered the house uninvited. While "standing behind him at his feet, weeping, she began to wet his feet with her tears, and wiped them with the hair of her head, and kissed his feet, and anointed them with the ointment" (Luke 7:38). Jesus seemed to have known the woman — to have been her "friend" — as his later comments indicate. This was perhaps her justification for boldly entering the house. In the eyes of the Pharisee, however, it was scandalous for a woman of questionable reputation to come into his home uninvited. Aligning himself with the woman, Jesus rebuked the Pharisee, whose name was Simon. Simon, said Jesus, offered no water to wash his feet; the woman used tears of love. Simon did not show any affection by greeting Jesus with a kiss; the woman kissed his feet. Simon did not even anoint his guest with olive oil (a cheap substance); the woman used perfume. Simon had not acted discourteously (neither water nor a kiss were demanded of a host in Jesus' day, though both were commonly given). But neither had Simon shown any real respect and affection — any real friendship — for Jesus. It is small wonder that Jesus preferred the woman to Simon.

Jesus' association with undesirables, the "tax collectors and harlots," is also suggested in Matthew 21:31-32, where Jesus asserts that it is such people who will enter the Kingdom of God (cf. Luke 19:1-10, the account concerning Zacchaeus, the tax collector; and John 8:2-11, the account of the woman caught in adultery). The scandalous nature of such friendships as judged by the larger populace testifies to their authenticity. Since it sought legitimacy for the Gospel, the early church scarcely would have invented such slander. Jesus was, in the words of I. H. Marshall, a "living parable" — "one who brought to sinners the offer of divine forgiveness and friendship."[77] Through the "new rules" he lived out in the time he spent with others, Jesus mirrored the freedom and joy characteristic of our life with God.

In addition to the Lukan account of the washing of Jesus' feet, there is a second "anointing" of Jesus by a friend which is recorded in the other Gospels. The incident took place in Bethany, sometime later in Jesus' life. Although the details of the story differ, depending on the emphasis of the particular Gospel writer, it is reported in Matthew, Mark, and John (Matt. 26:6-13, Mark 14:3-9, John 12:1-8).[78] Like the previous washing, this incident raised strong objections, this time from Jesus' disciples. They claimed that the costly ointment used might better have been sold and the proceeds given to the poor.

The accounts in Matthew and Mark are not concerned with identifying the woman, but John identifies her as Mary, Jesus' close friend. Moreover, John mentions that Martha and Lazarus, Mary's sister and brother, were also present, suggesting a warm, friendly dinner party as the occasion for the generous and loving act. As if to highlight the importance of Mary's friendship, both

Mark and John contrast her act with the deeds of Judas Iscariot (Mark 14:10, John 12:4). He would betray Jesus for money; she would lavish expensive oil on Jesus.

During Jesus' earthly ministry, many plotted against him (cf. Mark 14:1-2, 10-11). Mary was a welcome contrast, accepting him as he was, wanting to be with him, and lavishing gifts upon him (Mark 14:3-9). The Gospels of Mark and Matthew put the contrast in starkest terms, as they bracket their description of Mary's anointing with the sinister designs of the chief priests and scribes, and of Judas. Mary's acts showed both humility and affection. She was Jesus' friend. (In this context it is worth noting Kant's description of friendship as that which combines affection and respect.[79]) Thus Mary washed Jesus' feet (an act of humility) and used her hair to wipe off the excess ointment, or oil (an act of personal caring).

One further account concerning Jesus' pattern of friendship must also be mentioned. It, too, concerns Mary. In Luke 10, we read again of Jesus coming to Bethany to share a meal with Mary and Martha, this time at their home. Martha meant to honor her friend by preparing an elaborate meal. Mary chose instead to sit at his feet and listen to him. In a culture in which women had little significance beyond the kitchen, Mary's action was radical indeed. Moreover, as the immediate context of the dinner was Jesus' travels, Martha was correct in seeking to be hospitable. But it was the very need of providing hospitality that prevented Martha from listening to Jesus. The Greek text is ambiguous regarding Jesus' response. His reply might be, "few things are needful," i.e., keep the meal simple. Or more probably it is "one thing is needful," i.e., to listen to him takes priority. Although the latter interpretation is usually adopted, it is too often spiritualized, i.e., to sit at *Jesus'* feet is the one thing we need. Such an interpretation misses the point. It fails to see how important friendly conversation was to Jesus. I. H. Marshall goes so far as to suggest, following E. Laland, that the story was used in the early church to give instruction to women entertaining travelers.[80] Hospitality should involve more than a sumptuous banquet. It should also include friendly attention. It should be an occasion for enjoyment—for play—and not merely a duty.

Bonhoeffer's perceptive remarks, quoted earlier in part, are again appropriate:

> Who is there . . . in our times, who can devote himself . . . to
> . . . friendship. . . . Surely not the "ethical" man, but only the Chris-
> tian. Just because friendship belongs to this sphere of freedom
> ("of the Christian man"?!), it must be confidently defended against
> all the disapproving frowns of 'ethical' existences, though without
> claiming for it the *necessitas* of a divine decree, but only the
> *necessitas* of *freedom*. I believe that within the sphere of this
> freedom friendship is by far the rarest and most priceless treasure,
> for where else does it survive in this world of ours, dominated as
> it is by the *three other* mandates [marriage, work, state]? It cannot
> be compared with the treasures of the mandates, for in relation
> to them it is *sui generis*; it belongs to them as the cornflower
> belongs to the cornfield.[81]

The friendship of Mary, like the friendly act of the sinful woman,
cannot be compared with the obligation to provide one's guest
with food and drink or with the need to help the poor. Here was
Martha's error; here also the mistake of Jesus' critics. The obligation to work for justice remained paramount to Jesus. (Jesus,
you remember, defined his mission as being " 'to preach good
news to the poor . . . to proclaim release to the captives and
recovering of sight to the blind' "; Luke 4:18.) But alongside
Christ's work was his play, belonging to it "as the cornflower
belongs to the cornfield."

Conclusion

The evidence for "play" in the Bible is extensive. Yet we
have for the most part failed to recognize it or act upon it because our work-dominated culture has biased our interpretation.
We have questioned how a book as cynical and pessimistic as
Ecclesiastes could have found its way into the canon, failing to
see the text's central affirmation of our work and play as gifts
from God to be enjoyed. We have mistakenly interpreted the
Song of Songs to be about God's love for his people, unable to
consider that it could actually be a song in praise of lovers at
play. We have limited the Sabbath to that necessary pause that
refreshes, failing to understand its prior rationale as reflecting
the pattern of God himself. We have failed to note the playful
counterpoint that festival and feasting, music and dance provided—and are meant to provide. Somehow such descriptions

and commands have been thought of as relevant only to the ancient cult and no longer of concern to the Christian Church. We have failed to see their function to be that of surprising us with joy. We have understood the Old Testament custom of hospitality solely in ethical terms, viewing it as necessary for a traveler's well-being but failing to note also its wider context in play. We have overlooked the importance of simple friendship to Jesus, interpreting kindnesses to him in terms of his role as Savior. In all of these ways we have been guilty of misunderstanding the biblical record. As Christians we have failed to let Scripture speak authoritatively to us about our need to play.

V

Work:
Its Relationship to Play

THE COUNTERPOINT OF ANY DISCUSSION OF THE Christian at play is a treatment of the Christian at work. It is this fact that lies behind our discussion of contemporary work practices in Chapter One. It is this recognition that also informs my criticisms of both Sam Keen and Jurgen Moltmann in Chapter Three. In our biblical discussion in Chapter Four, particularly with regard to Qoheleth's advice and in reference to a theology of the Sabbath, the necessity of viewing work and play together is again evident. Qoheleth sets before his readers a vision of men and women both enjoying their play and giving themselves fully to their work. Such a complementary perspective is central to the idea of the Sabbath as well, the day of rest flooding our other six days of work with its light.

To view the Christian at play from a final vantage point, and to illustrate the necessary hermeneutical circulation between culture, tradition, and biblical text, let us briefly return to the relationship of play and work, this time from the perspective of a Christian understanding of work. If our contemporary culture has wrongly influenced Christian thinking about work (and play), how can a fresh assessment of the biblical sources be used to counter this trend? Can a theology of work (as well as a theology of play) be used to address the problem of leisure facing countless Americans?

The Christian at Work

A brief sketch of the Bible's description of work shows clearly its importance for the Christian. While many of Israel's neighbors relegated hard work to the women, the slaves, and the laboring class, Israel recognized that work was from the beginning God's purpose for humankind (Gen. 1:26, Ps. 104:19-24, Isa. 28:23-29, Eccl. 3:22: ". . . there is nothing better than that a man should enjoy his work, for that is his lot"). Although work's hardships are understood as a divine curse invoked on account of sin (Gen. 3:17-19), work itself is taken for granted biblically; it is basic to humankind (e.g., Ps. 65; 67). The biblical writers recognize that idolatry (Luke 12:16-22) and exploitation (Jas. 5:4) are too often the result of work, but work in itself is the God-ordained form for service within the community (cf. Isa. 41:6-7, Eph. 6:5-9) which is intended to bring glory to God (Col. 3:17). Certainly it is worthy of its reward (Luke 10:7).

The Christian is both created for and called to work. How does this fact bear upon one's existence also as player? The prophet Amos provides a starting point for our discussion in his reflection on Israel's unethical work practices as they related to her observance of the Sabbath. According to this Old Testament prophet, the Sabbath in pre-exilic Israel became an offense to God (Amos 8:1-6). As observed by the Israelites in the eighth century, the Sabbath was denied its role of transforming and enlightening the remainder of the week — the Israelites' six days of work. Although the Sabbath participants outwardly "played" — although they observed the religious practices and refrained from work — their activity was not truly playful, relativizing and refreshing their larger world. Instead, the Israelites' "work" assumed a false priority, so much so that when the Sabbath was over, the poor were again cheated and the needy oppressed.

Unwilling to allow their Sabbath experience to be truly play because of their equal unwillingness to let their work be that which God intended, the Israelites of Amos's day chafed under the Sabbath restrictions. Rather than enjoying their time-with-others in freedom before God, the Israelites reduced the meaning of their Sabbath play to mandatory work stoppages (and, perhaps, the opportunity for immoral excess; cf. Amos 1:7-8, 5:21-24). This lifeless shell of inauthentic play proved unattractive. It is hardly surprising that the Israelites waited expectantly for their playtimes (the observation of the new moon and the Sabbath) to end, so they could get back to the business at hand of maximizing their profits. Faulty work and faulty play went together.

Here is Amos's description:

> Hear this, you who trample upon the needy,
>   and bring the poor of the land to an end,
> saying, "When will the new moon be over,
>   that we may sell grain?
> And the sabbath,
>   that we may offer wheat for sale,
> that we may make the ephah small and the shekel great,
>   and deal deceitfully with false balances,
> that we may buy the poor for silver
>   and the needy for a pair of sandals,
>   and sell the refuse of the wheat?" (Amos 8:4-6)

Amos responded to the inauthentic work and play of his day by speaking God's word of judgment upon his people. Amos cried out that God hated their feasts and the noise of their songs. He said God refused to listen any longer to the melody of their harps, for justice and righteousness had been forsaken in their work (Amos 5:21-24). Moreover, God would turn these songs into lamentation and would transform any riches into famine (Amos 8:9-12). The Israelites had lost their ability to "work" authentically, Amos observed, and with it their ability to "play" authentically, too.

The prophet's insights are applicable to our day as well. Social scientists point out that when work sours, play does too.[1] In particular, when people spend their working days at jobs primarily to earn the money that will permit them to enjoy the remainder of life, they often discover they are unable to give themselves fully to their play. As Kenneth Keniston observes: "Life is of a piece, and if work is empty or routine [or evil], the rest will inevitably become contaminated as well."[2] Perhaps the most obvious example of this in society today is the appeal of mass entertainment—whether television, movies, or sports. Requiring little discipline on the part of the audience and offering a vicarious sense of achievement and personal freedom, often with an overlay of gratuitous violence and sex, our mass entertainment becomes all too often "a pathetically misguided search for those values of personal existence which are so evidently absent from daily labor in the everexpanding networks of technology. . . ."[3] With mass labor proving unfulfilling to many, their play becomes a vain attempt to live as human beings.

The challenge facing the Christian, then, is not merely the

recovery of one's play. It is also the reconstitution of one's work (see Chapter One). Play and work go together. When work is without meaning, all of life suffers. When work is put in its God-intended perspective, however, authentic play tends to follow naturally.

Bernard Mergen's study of work and play among American shipyard workers provides an example. Mergen observes that over the last sixty years practical jokes on the job have decreased proportionately with the workers' pride in craftsmanship. According to Mergen,

> In the 1930's a man would go down into an unlighted area of a ship with portable lights only to find that someone had unplugged his cord at the switchbox as a joke. Apprentices were sometimes sent for nonexistent tools, such as a flag pole key. Retired workers think that this kind of play on the job has declined in recent years . . . partly because younger workers are less deeply involved in their crafts.[4]

As a person works, so he tends to play.

The Relationship of Work and Play: Five Possible Models

In a paper presented to the Sixth World Congress of Sociology, Kunio Odaka classified several thousand workers in Japanese industry according to their preferences among "five types of living related to work and leisure [play]."[5] These possibilities were defined as follows:

1. *Work-oriented-unilateral*: "Work is man's duty. I wish to devote myself wholly to my work without any thought of leisure."

2. *Leisure-oriented-unilateral*: "Work is no more than a means for living. The enjoyment of leisure is what makes human life worth living."

3. *Identity*: "There is no distinction between work and leisure. I therefore have no need of being liberated from work in order that I may enjoy leisure."

4. *Split*: "Work is work and leisure is leisure. Modern man gets his work done smartly, and enjoys his leisure moderately."

5. *Integrated*: "Work makes leisure pleasurable, and leisure gives new energy to work. I wish to work with all my might, and to enjoy leisure."

Odaka discovered that the majority of those interviewed favored the "integrated" pattern in which work and leisure are complementary. He also discovered, paradoxically, that among these same workers, only 6-14 percent actually found their work balanced by their play; 25-47 percent found their play more important in making their "life worth living," and 36-56 percent found their home life the more significant factor. That is, although an "integrated" pattern was the ideal, in reality a "leisure-oriented-unilateral" pattern was the norm.

Odaka's classification of workers' viewpoints is useful because it summarizes five options open to the American Christian in relating work to play. It also cautions us that the ideal, the "right" answers do not always match one's experience. We have already discussed several of Odaka's options. In our discussion of a biblical model of play, for example, as well as in our description of the theologies of Jurgen Moltmann and Sam Keen, we considered the first two of Odaka's types: the work-oriented and the leisure-oriented models. Labeled the "Protestant" and the "Greek" models, these options were shown to divorce work and play by denying the efficacy of one or the other. In this context the "Hebraic" model was presented as the seldom adopted yet biblical alternative. If one now considers these work-play relationships more directly from the perspective of work, it becomes even clearer why Christians have failed to understand a truly biblical anthropology concerning their play. For both "Protestant" and "Greek" models have behind them rich and ongoing Christian traditions concerning work as well.

The "Protestant" ("work-oriented-unilateral") tradition has been well documented by those like Weber and Tawney, even if its origins have been wrongly attributed to Calvin himself. Dorothy Sayers, the poet and writer of detective stories, states the position clearly in *Creed or Chaos?*: "Work is not, primarily, a thing one does to live, but the thing one lives to do."[6] Sayers believes she is solving the problem of work in contemporary society by opposing Odaka's "split" paradigm. In reality she is merely restating an alternate and more prevalent problem: the Protestant over-valuation of work. (She is also undercutting the intended joy one might receive from reading her stories about Lord Peter Wimsey, that remarkable detective. Need such reading be simply escapist? Surely not.) Work, which is meant to be part of life, often threatens to consume the whole of life.

Moreover, when work becomes one's sole focus, its nature as vocation (as "calling," *vocare,* from God) is easily denied, work for its own sake becoming wrongly equated with service to God. As George Forell comments: "We find here the position that faithfulness in our job saves us, that the life of Christian discipleship is achieved when we are [simply] good shoemakers, good butchers, good teachers, good welders, good pastors, and last, but by no means least, good bankers."[7] For us as Christians, work is never the central measure of our worth. In Christ we are children of God and are fully accepted as such. From the perspective of Christ's birth, death, and resurrection, we simply do not need to worry about our worth based on the success of our endeavors. We need only be faithful to our calling.

Identifying God's blessing with success in our work is a particularly Protestant problem, though it is not without its Catholic practitioners. Each Sunday the airwaves are filled with this gospel of success. Christianity and successful, decent work are all too glibly associated by politicians and preachers alike. "It pays to be a Christian." "God wants you to be a success." George Forell is again to the point when he rebukes such shallowness: "The worship of the self-made man has no room in a church which believes that we are God-made men."[8]

If Wittenberg and Geneva have tended to turn work into an end in itself, Rome has at times been tempted by the converse, seeing work chiefly as an evil to be tolerated as necessary. Influenced by "Greek" thought, some Catholics have misread the Genesis accounts of Creation and the Fall, understanding work to be a consequence of sin (cf. Karl Rahner).[9] What has been overlooked is that God's command to both male and female to have dominion over the earth, to cultivate and take care of the garden, predates the Fall and its resultant curse upon humankind's endeavors. This "Greek" misreading of work squares with Odaka's second "work-play" category, the "leisure-oriented-unilateral" model. Contemplation, not activity, becomes our goal; the monastery, not the workbench, the place.

While such a Christian understanding of work (and play) is historically to be identified with one branch of Catholicism, it is not limited to any branch of the Church. Horace Bushnell, for example, arguably the leading nineteenth-century Protestant theologian in the field of Christian education, held to a similar position. In his Phi Beta Kappa Speech in 1848, he argued that the signs of work are offensive to the Christian, revealing some "defect or insufficiency." To say that a person *labors* is the same as to say that he or she fails. "Nothing is sufficient or great, nothing fires or exalts us," he claimed, "but to feel the divine energy and the inspiring liberty of play." Bushnell is one of our "Greek" workers, for whom toil is at best a temporary evil, "having for its end the realization of a state of play."[10]

Here, then, are two traditional Christian (mis) understandings of our work vis-à-vis our play. Two other of Odaka's options deserve mention as well—though they are also deficient—because they are attracting increasing numbers of Christians who are sensitive to the inadequacies of traditional theological formulations. Some would argue today that work and play need not be distinguished. Instead, one must learn to work playfully (or play "workfully"). Here is Odaka's "identity" paradigm. Other Christians would oppose any such equation as simplistic, claiming that work is work and play is play. The two have no connection. In fact, it is argued, they are actually at cross-purposes. Given such a condition, a person must balance the two off against each other as best he or she can. Here is Odaka's "split" paradigm.

The merging of work and play—the "identity" model—is the particular temptation of the satisfied Christian worker (the executive, carpenter, pastor, or professor who is easily captured by work's challenges). For such people, play is increasingly disguised as work and vice versa. Sales executives talk to customers on the golf course and bank presidents have their private dining rooms. Ministers sponsor Christian tours to Hawaii. Today the lines between our work and our play are frequently blurred. Some social theorists, like Yankelovich, see this as laudable. But we have already observed the central danger within this fusion (and confusion) of work and play in our discussion of the Sabbath. The Sabbath, that time carefully set apart from the ongoing concerns of work, was meant to relativize the efforts of those who found work intoxicating. It was intended to remind the worker that she or he is not God. When play and work are muddled, the impact of play is diminished because it is experienced halfheartedly and superficially. The result is an undervaluing of play's rightful place in life and a further compromising of play's needed autonomy. The intermingling of work and play may seem to make work more enjoyable, but it also takes away much of play's helpful consequence.

Similar cautions against the merger of work and play can be addressed from the standpoint of work. Scripture is cautious in affirming our "creative" work, for it all too easily becomes idolatrous. As Alan Richardson states, "Indeed, there is throughout the Bible an underlying suspicion of anything approaching admiration of 'the works of men's hands' (Ps. 115:4; Isa. 40:18ff.; 44:9ff.) . . . admiration of the creative faculty in man may lead to a non-biblical humanism which exalts the creature rather than the Only-Creator. The biblical writers will have none of it."[11] There are other potential problems as well. Playful work, for example, often masks a sense of guilt which drives perpetual workers. Unable to accept themselves, such workers compensate by becoming "cheerful" workaholics. Their last desire is to find themselves idle at the beach or in the mountains. Work is truly apotheosized.

The divorcing of work and play—the "split" model—is more typical of the common worker, one who at times despairs of finding meaning in or through his job. Sympathetic to the plight of many such Christian workers, Sherwood Wirt sets work and play in tension. He recalls the well-worn story of three men laboring on a medieval cathedral, who say respectively in answer to a query about what they are doing: "I am chipping these stones"; "I am earning my wages"; and "I am building a cathedral." Traditionally the third answer has been held up as the ideal, the dignity of work as vocation thereby being recognized. Wirt, however, quotes approvingly from Emil Brunner: "I would prefer to be the second man, emphasizing my wages which help to support my family." Concludes Wirt, "The labor market in our country being what it is, it would be well for us to think carefully before we put the concept of Christian vocation 'in overalls' . . . and set it to work. Luther's dairymaid could possibly have 'milked to the glory of God' although we have only the preacher's word for it, not the dairymaid's."[12]

Wirt is right to protest against the romanticizing of the workplace. Nevertheless, a biblical notion of Christian vocation will have nothing to do with such compartmentalization and secularization. We are to cultivate the crops that God has planted for our sustenance. Our work is to model his, producing "food from the earth, and wine to gladden the heart of man" (Ps. 104:14). By working, we not only fulfill one aspect of our God-intended humanity (Gen. 1:26, Eccl. 2:24) but also serve the community by providing both necessities and things of pleasure ("food" and "wine"), thereby bringing glory to God our maker.

Wirt is sensitive to the drudgery that characterizes much work today. But one must realize that the humdrum has always been a major ingredient of work: it was so in Luther's day, and even in biblical times. As Bengt Hoffman observes, "It is not a modern discovery that life is to a considerable extent necessary habit and unglamorous repetition. ... A realistic view of the doctrine of creation should make us less eager to concede that 'depersonalization' is the only evaluative word we can use about work via the machine and in the business organization."[13] God is the Lord of the world of automation as well. Antoine de Saint-Exupery has aptly expressed my criticism of the "split" paradigm: "It is using a pick-ax to no purpose that makes a prison." Rather than separate the work arena from the Christian's larger sphere of meaning, we—as wives, children, fathers, and workers—are to "do all to the glory of God." "Whatever your task," writes Paul, "work heartily, as serving the Lord and not men, knowing that from the Lord you will receive the inheritance as your reward; you are serving the Lord Christ" (Col. 3:17-24).

Work and Play as Complementary

Rather than spend all our time at work (the "identity" model) or defensively protect our time for play (the "split" model), we as Christians need to revere time for both work and play. This involves the remaining work-play model, the "integrated" paradigm. We are to work with all our might, and to enjoy our play, for "God has already approved what [we] do" (Eccl. 9:7-10). This, as I have argued in the preceding chapter, is the consistent biblical witness. Gerard Manley Hopkins has expressed it well:

Smiting on an anvil, sawing a beam, white-washing a wall, driving horses, sweeping, scouring, everything gives God some glory if being in His grace you do it as your duty. To go to Communion worthily gives God great glory, but to take food in thankfulness and temperance gives Him glory too. To lift up the hands in prayer gives God glory, but a man with a dungfork in his hand, a woman with a slop pail, give Him glory too. He is so great that all things give Him glory if you mean they should. So then, my brethren, live.[14]

Our central task as Christians is not to maximize either our work or our play while minimizing the other, nor to merge our work with our play. Instead, Christians are created and called to consecrate both their work and their play. As we have seen, play is God's appointment, his gift to humankind which is meant to relativize and refresh our endeavors, putting them in their God-intended perspective. But work too is from God, his appointed means of service to "man" and nature alike.

In his essay "Theology and the Playful Life," Lewis Smedes buttresses our argument for an "integrated" work-play paradigm by appealing to the work-oriented perspective of his own Calvinistic tradition. Smedes finds that even within the "anti-play theology" of his own church, even within its theological summons to work, there is hidden a concomitant invitation to play. Although God instructs us to be sober and vigilant stewards, he also likens us to children singing and dancing.

Smedes chooses three basic tenets of his Reformed faith to illustrate both the Calvinists' seeming antipathy to play and their actual playfulness underlying that. First, in a world governed by God, all is destined. While affirming this article of faith, Smedes suggests that the freedom of God's grace to respond to human sin in a benevolent way indicates that everything is also surprising. Understood in this context, play mirrors the freedom and adventure of God himself; it becomes a parable of the surprising reality of grace. Play has its place even in God's "controlled universe." Secondly, Smedes says, the Christian theology of sin would seem to preclude the world of the player—sin being such dreadfully straightforward business. But sin also causes us not to take ourselves too seriously. In grace we discover that we need not take sin with absolute seriousness because God has done so for us. We are free also to play.

Thirdly, Smedes writes, the doctrine of vocation, when viewed from the perspective of work alone, would remove the purposeless from life and thus eliminate man's playfulness. In the Reformed tradition, "Office means duty. Duty means work.

Work . . . is the privilege given creatures of serving under their Great Taskmaster's eye." Furthermore, the seriousness of our vocation is intensified by our limits, our finitude. Within the Reformed tradition we are encouraged to "redeem the time," to "work for the night is coming." But the Christian has another "vocation" — a gracious calling — to *be* as well as to do, to become as well as to produce. The shortness of life has another message too: that our efforts will never be sufficient to save us, so we must trust God and his grace.[15] Smedes concludes, "Every facet of our theological ethos that summons us to work has an invitation to play snuggled inside of it."[16]

As Smedes describes it, grace is the hidden element in each of these otherwise work-producing doctrines of the Church. Without grace, without a recognition that all of life rests in the hands of a playful God, everything becomes either "despairingly serious or playfully illusionary." "It is burdensome," writes Smedes, "to be serious without grace, for then one has to be serious without relief. But then, too, without grace, playfulness becomes an escape from seriousness."[17] God's grace transforms the over-earnestness and routine of our work. It allows us to participate fully in what is, by grace, no longer an ultimately serious endeavor. Moreover, grace lies behind our summons to play as well. We have, for example, been created as sexual beings intended to mirror a God of love. We have also been commanded to honor the Lord's Day by not working but playing. There is, in short, a God-ordained and graciously upheld rhythm of work and play that we are called to adopt. However obscured and distorted it has become today, this pattern is nevertheless basic to life itself, a refraction of the image of God in which we are made.

An "integrated" work-play model can be strongly argued for, both from the biblical record and, surprisingly, from the Reformed tradition itself, that most "Protestant" of Christian theologies. This model is also beginning to be recognized by a few in secular society as that paradigm most conducive to human well-being. Such a rhythm is being suggested as a solution to our current unrest both as individuals and as a society: it is being proposed as a way of maximizing the human potential. At present, the advocates are few. Nevertheless, they are provocative because they provide contemporary cultural support for this biblical-traditional model. The sage advice of Old Testament wisdom writers is increasingly being echoed today. (Here is yet another example of the possible and necessary hermeneutical circulation between culture, tradition, and biblical text.) Basing their conclusions on observations of people who live successfully, such writers as George Vaillant, Jay Rohrlich, and Charles Garfield are arguing for a necessary and crucial balance between our work and our play.

Vaillant's book, *Adaptation to Life,* reports on the findings of a study of several hundred Harvard University graduates who were interviewed over a forty-year period from their undergraduate days into their middle age. Vaillant's interest was in "the kinds of people who do well and are well." His conclusion: being a good businessman goes hand in hand with being a good tennis player and husband. Contrary to common mythology, the very men who enjoyed the best marriages and the richest friendships tended also to become the company presidents. "Inner happiness, external play, objective vocational success, mature inner defenses, good outward marriage, all correlate highly—not perfectly, but at least as powerfully as height correlates with weight."[18] There are exceptions to any observation about life, as the writer of Ecclesiastes reminds us forcefully. But like Qoheleth's observation that we should enjoy both our work and our play, Vaillant recognizes the value of a balanced life.

Similar findings have been made by Jay Rohrlich, a practicing psychiatrist with an office on Wall Street. In his book *Work and Love: The Crucial Balance,* he argues from a Freudian perspective that "working and loving [which is for him the essence of play] are states of mind. The quality of our lives depends on a healthy balance between them."[19] The same conclusion has been reached by Charles Garfield, a psychologist at the University of California Medical School in San Francisco. In 1967 Garfield launched a nationwide study to find out why some people are very successful workers and others are not. Although the workaholic might initially outdistance the others, Garfield discovered such a person not to be the "optimal performer," the one making the major contribution in any group, profession, or business. In analyzing five major groups (athletes, educators, health-care workers, creative artists, and people in business and industry), Garfield discovered that the high performers (those recognized as being in the forefront by their colleagues) had a work style that could be characterized by "intention and delight." In contrast with all others—the workaholic, who worked "with determination and for relief," being the most extreme—high-level performers had a sense of joy about their activities.

Moreover, almost without exception the most successful people not only worked hard but played with equal intensity. Furthermore, if their work was chiefly physical, they turned in their play to something cerebral (e.g., athletes often enjoyed meditation or reading). If their work involved management positions in which they were in control, they enjoyed in their play something that required an acceptance of life as it presented itself, e.g., bird watching or sailing. (Very few optimal performers in business had motorboats.) Garfield's conclusion: "There is a kind of reflexive balancing, or equilibrium, around which the optimal performer launches his or her efforts. There is a centeredness if you will."[20]

The style of life God intended for us includes both work and play in a creative rhythm, and its value is observable even by those who do not make use of the Scriptures. Although God has not created all of us to be "optimal performers" by society's standards, he has revealed an optimal pattern for human life more generally, one that is consistent with observations of successful living ("general revelation") and with Scriptural truth ("special revelation"). As Christians we are not only to play—we are to work. But we are also not only to work—we are to play.

Conclusion

AMONG THOSE WHO HAD THE PRIVILEGE OF KNOWING him personally, Dietrich Bonhoeffer is remembered not first of all for his theology but for his humanity. It is his life that has given import to his thought.[1] This assessment is also true for many people like me, who never knew him but have read both his theology and his biography. It is his life which speaks with almost singular force.

When one thinks of Bonhoeffer, the story of his martyrdom under Hitler immediately comes to mind. The freedom of single-minded obedience to Christ which characterized his life on behalf of others continues to be a powerful model for countless Christians. But Bonhoeffer the man was more than his final act of martyrdom, more even than his courageous service as theologian and churchman. His personality had other sides, perhaps as significant as the ones that are highlighted. Bonhoeffer's ethical stance (his being a "man for others") was complemented by his equally developed aesthetic posture (his existence as a "man with others").

In a volume of personal reminiscences by his friends entitled *I Knew Dietrich Bonhoeffer,* time and again Bonhoeffer's play is remembered alongside his work. Those who knew him recall his ability at tennis and Ping-Pong, his unfailing sense of humor, his love of ethnic foods, and his piano-playing and evenings spent listening to chamber music. His acquaintances recall his love for Goethe, for cultured table-talk, travel, and singing. For example, Wolf-Dieter Zimmermann writes, "Bonhoeffer was generous with money. He wanted to enjoy what gave him pleasure. He loved the theatre and cinema, music, good food and drink, travel and fashionable clothes. He wanted others to share these things too; he did not want to enjoy them in secret."[2]

Seeking to understand the profound influence which Bonhoeffer had upon him, Albrecht Schönherr, one of Bonhoeffer's students at the Confessing Church's Seminary in Finkenwalde, reflects:

> What was it that fascinated us young people in Bonhoeffer? Nothing particular: his appearance was imposing but not elegant; his voice high, but not rich; his formulations were laborious, not brilliant. Perhaps it was that here we met a quite single-hearted, or in the words of Matthew VI, 22, a "sound man."

Schönherr goes on to develop his thesis about Bonhoeffer's "sound" life. He was not a one-sided intellectual. Bonhoeffer the theologian argued for the idea of "deputyship," our responsibility in Christ for our fellow man. And Bonhoeffer the Christian therefore "staked his life for the liberation of Germany and the world from the curse of murderous tyranny." He gave his all to other pursuits as well. His students were somewhat embarrassed that he, their elder and a townsman to boot, could outrun them in all the ballgames at Finkenwalde. Among the highlights were those times when Bonhoeffer played a piano concerto by Beethoven. So too were the half-hour of meditation and the time of silence which he made the discipline of the entire seminary community: "A unifying arch swung from music and play to quietude and prayer. . . ." Schönherr concludes his brief reflection by admitting to being "under the spell of that man who gave himself so entirely, heart and soul, whether in play or in theological discussion."[3]

Just prior to his arrest and imprisonment, Bonhoeffer wrote a brief essay entitled "After Ten Years." He sent it to a few friends as a Christmas present in 1942. Knowing that his arrest was likely and experiencing the horror of wartime Germany, he asked the question, "Who stands fast?" His answer, "Only the man whose final standard is not his reason, his principles, his conscience, his freedom, or his virtue . . . (only) the responsible man, who tries to make his whole life an answer to the question and call of God." Such a call would involve the Christian in sympathy and action on behalf of those who were suffering, for whose sake Christ also suffered. Moreover, such "courage to enter public life" would be matched by continuing "pleasure in private life." Bonhoeffer called for a "return from the newspaper and the radio to the book, from feverish activity to unhurried leisure, from dispersion to concentration, from sensationalism to reflection, from virtuosity to art, from snobbery to modesty, from extravagance to moderation." Such a concern for the playful side of life did not compromise his participation in the Church struggle—it enhanced it. "Quantities are competitive," he wrote; "qualities are complementary."[4]

This "sound" life, which developed in freedom, continued even during Bonhoeffer's prison years. In his letters written from captivity we read of his continued work in theological study, reflection, and writing. He was constantly requesting new books to read. Moreover, his letters and papers from prison, which were published posthumously, document that this period was indeed a time of productivity. Many, in fact, would argue that his prison writings are among the most significant theological works of the last fifty years.

But Bonhoeffer's letters and papers reveal more than the continuing fertility of a theological mind; they give evidence of an ongoing balance in his personal life. While in prison, Bonhoeffer read many stories and novels just for fun. He loved to hear music from the guard's radio but would criticize what struck him as banal. He sang hymns and *lieder*. He played chess and/or worked solitary chess problems by the hour. He followed the church year in his private worship. He read his Bible devotionally, particularly the Old Testament. He detested gossip but loved to talk with two or three people. By letter he engaged his friend, Eberhard Bethge, in discussion about landscape painting and requested his reaction to Michelangelo's *Pietà*. Bonhoeffer even began to write his own stories and poems, and started work on a novel.

For Bonhoeffer, the Christian life was a combination of work and play, of Church and culture, of solitude and time spent with others. Such a pattern could not be split up or dismembered; its rhythm had a continuous flow. As he himself commented, "A common denominator must be sought both in thought and in a personal and integrated attitude to life."[5] Bonhoeffer reflected on this fact on several occasions during his stay in prison. Recalling the story of a certain young man, for example, he wrote:

> We read that he set out into the world "*um das Ganze zu tun*" (to do the whole thing); here we have the *ánthrōpos téleios* (*téleios* originally meant 'whole' in the sense of 'complete' or 'perfect'); 'you, therefore, must be perfect (*téleios*), as your heavenly

Father is perfect' (Matt. 5.48) — in contrast to the *anḗr dípsychos* ('a double-minded man') of James 1.8.[6]

To "do the whole thing," to be a whole man — an *ánthrōpos téleios* — such was Bonhoeffer's desire. He realized, however, that apart from some integrating principle — or, better, apart from some integrator — life's wholeness would prove illusory.

From his prison cell Bonhoeffer reflected on life's centeredness in God, which allows for its concomitant diversity. Turning to the metaphor of music, he said there is a "polyphony of life." He wrote:

> What I mean is that God wants us to love him eternally with our whole hearts — not in such a way as to injure or weaken our earthly love, but to provide a kind of *cantus firmus* to which the other melodies of life provide the counterpoint. One of these contrapuntal themes (which have their own complete independence but are yet related to the *cantus firmus*) is earthly affection. Even in the Bible we have the Song of Songs; and really one can imagine no more ardent, passionate, sensual love than is portrayed there (see 7:6). It is a good thing that that book is in the Bible, in face of all those who believe that the restraint of passion is Christian. (Where is there such restraint in the Old Testament?) Where the *cantus firmus* is clear and plain, the counterpoint can be developed to its limits.

Bonhoeffer concluded that "only a polyphony of this kind can give life a wholeness and at the same time assure us that nothing calamitous can happen as long as the *cantus firmus* is kept going."[7]

Bonhoeffer's concern for wholeness in life — for faithfulness to Christ in both his work and his play — was evident even during his prison years. It was particularly apparent in the care he took to nurture his friendships. For him, friendship was one manifestation of culture. It could not be classified as work, a categorization some Lutherans were prone to make. It belonged not to the sphere of obedience but to that broad arena of freedom. Bonhoeffer counseled, "The man who is ignorant of this area of freedom may be a good father, citizen, and worker, indeed even a Christian; but I doubt whether he is a complete man and therefore a Christian in the widest sense of the term."[8]

The making of a complete man or woman — "a Christian in the widest sense of the term" — has been the larger purpose of this book. With our time increasing for friendship and for art, for reading and for tennis, and with our need for such play perhaps stronger than ever before, given the nature of our work, the question facing both the Church and our wider culture is why our practice of play remains so filled with problems. Why is it that our potentially playful experiences have all too often been turned into attempted escapes from tension or boredom, or beyond that, into exercises geared to accomplish something?

It is my thesis that what is presently wrong in American life centers in our continuing attitude as a people. Our work-dominated value scheme and our reigning technocracy have obscured our vision of life's full possibilities. In this situation the Christian Church could serve a prophetic role within the wider society — if it only would. Unfortunately, Christian theologians have scarcely fared better than general society in understanding the necessity of a balanced life. Some have included play within their work agendas, while others have made play central to their mission of self-fulfillment. But whether "play as politics" or "play as total ideology," the results have been similar: life has been reduced to something less than itself. We as a church do not know how to play.

In order to remove the blinders of our contemporary culture, we as Christians must listen afresh to the biblical witness. If we would only be attentive, we would hear Scripture proclaim that our play, like our work, is to be a God-given expression of our humanity. Along with our work, play is part of the intended rhythm for our lives. Such a viewpoint concerning play (and work) is heard not only in the Song of Songs (where Bonhoeffer recognized its presence) but in the biblical discussion of Sabbath rest. It is central to the book of Ecclesiastes, and is illustrated in Jesus' pattern of friendship. It is also basic to such Israelite practices as festival, dance, feasting, and the providing of hospitality.

Contrary to those who would understand play as merely general organic activity, we must understand play as a specific human event, one rooted both creationally and attitudinally. Dietrich Bonhoeffer is correct in realizing that in times like these, not everyone will be able to play — "surely not the 'ethical' man, but only the Christian." The true Christian, Bonhoeffer writes, should appreciate the "cornflower" as well as the "cornfield":

Beside the cornfield that sustains us,
tilled and cared for reverently by men
sweating as they labour at their task,
and, if need be, giving their life's blood —
beside the field that gives their daily bread
men also let the lovely cornflower thrive.
. . . .
Beside the staff of life,
taken and fashioned from the heavy earth,
beside our marriage, work, and war,
the free man, too, will live and grow towards the sun.
Not the ripe fruit alone —
blossom is lovely, too.
Does blossom only serve the fruit,
or does fruit only serve the blossom —
who knows?
But both are given to us.[9]

Notes

INTRODUCTION

1. Thomas Oden, *Agenda for Theology: Recovering Christian Roots* (San Francisco: Harper & Row, 1979), p. 22.
2. Thomas Oden, "The Human Potential and Evangelical Hope," *The Drew Gateway,* 24 (Fall 1972), 5.
3. *Ibid.,* p. 6.
4. Cf. David L. Miller, "Theology and Play Studies: An Overview," *Journal of the American Academy of Religion,* 39 (September 1971), 350.
5. William A. Sadler, Jr., "Creative Existence: Play as a Pathway to Personal Freedom and Community," *Humanitas,* 5 (Spring 1969), 57.
6. Augustine, *Confessions,* trans. F. J. Sheed (New York: Sheed & Ward, 1942), X, 31.
7. Robert K. Johnston, *Evangelicals at an Impasse: Biblical Authority in Practice* (Atlanta: John Knox Press, 1979), p. 150.
8. C. René Padilla, "Hermeneutics and Culture—A Theological Perspective," in *Down to Earth: Studies in Christianity and Culture,* ed. John R. W. Stott and Robert Coote (Grand Rapids, Mich.: Eerdmans, 1980), pp. 73, 75. Cf. Anthony C. Thiselton, *The Two Horizons: New Testament Hermeneutics and Philosophical Description* (Grand Rapids, Mich.: Eerdmans, 1980); C. René Padilla, "The Interpreted Word: Reflections on Contextual Hermeneutics," *Themelios,* 7 (September 1981), 18-23.

CHAPTER ONE—PLAY:
A PROBLEM FOR THE CONTEMPORARY PERSON

1. Joseph Zeisel, "The Workweek in American Industry, 1850-1956," in *Mass Leisure,* ed. Eric Larrabee and Rolf Meyersohn (Glencoe, Ill.: Free Press, 1958), pp. 145-153. It is interesting to note that when Thomas More published his *Utopia* in 1516, his "radical" vision called for a nine-hour workday and a sixty-hour workweek.
2. Staffan Burenstam Linder, *The Harried Leisure Class* (New York: Columbia University Press, 1970), p. 136.
3. Zeisel, "The Workweek in American Industry, 1850-1956," p. 151.
4. Marion Clawson, "How Much Leisure, Now and in the Future?", in *Leisure in America: Blessing or Curse?,* ed. James C. Charlesworth, Monograph 4 (Philadelphia: American Academy of Political and Social Science, 1964), p. 13.
5. U.S. Cong., Senate, Committee on Labor and Public Welfare, Subcommittee on Employment, Manpower, and Poverty, *Work in*

America, report of a special task force to the Secretary of Health, Education, and Welfare, 93rd Cong., 1st sess. (Washington, D.C.: GPO, 1973), p. 54.

6. *Ibid.,* pp. x-xi.

7. Studs Terkel, *Working* (New York: Random House, Pantheon Books, 1974), pp. xi-xxiv.

8. *Ibid.,* p. xxiv.

9. U.S. Cong., *Work in America,* p. 31.

10. Joseph Dumazedier, "Leisure and Post-Industrial Societies," in *Technology, Human Values and Leisure,* ed. Max Kaplan and Philip Bosserman (New York: Abingdon Press, 1971), pp. 194-195.

11. Richard M. Pfeffer, *Working for Capitali$m* (New York: Columbia University Press, 1979), p. 2. Cf. pp. 232-236.

12. Gordon J. Dahl, "Time and Leisure Today," *The Christian Century,* February 10, 1971, p. 187.

13. Francis R. Duffy, "Looking at a Leisure-Time Society," *Leisure Living,* Duquesne Community College Lecture Series I (Pittsburgh: Duquesne University, 1959), p. 46.

14. Josef Pieper, *Leisure: The Basis of Culture,* trans. Alexander Dru (New York: Random House, Pantheon Books, 1964), p. 27.

15. Clawson, "How Much Leisure?", p. 16.

16. Charles K. Brightbill, *Education for Leisure-Centered Living* (Harrisburg, Pa.: Stackpole Books, 1966), pp. 15-16.

17. Ralph Abernathy, "Leisure Time for the Poor," *Spectrum,* 48 (January/February 1972), 11-12, 14.

18. Daniel Yankelovich, *New Rules: Searching for Self-Fulfillment in a World Turned Upside Down* (New York: Random House, 1981), p. xv.

19. Cf. Betty Friedan, *The Second Stage* (New York: Summit Books, 1981).

20. Linder, *The Harried Leisure Class,* pp. 2-3.

21. *Ibid.,* p. 88.

22. Lyle Schaller, *The Impact of the Future* (New York: Abingdon Press, 1969), pp. 84-85.

23. Quoted in Russell Lynes, "Time on Our Hands," in *Mass Leisure,* p. 347.

24. Arthur Schlesinger, Jr., "Implications of Leisure," in *Technology, Human Values and Leisure,* p. 77.

25. Linder, *The Harried Leisure Class,* p. 101.

26. Max Kaplan, "The Relevancy of Leisure," in *Technology, Human Values and Leisure,* p. 22.

27. Lawrence F. Greenberger, "The Impact of More Leisure in a Capitalistic Economy," *Leisure Living,* p. 12.

28. Cf. M. Douglas Meeks, Introd., *Fest: The Transformation of Everyday,* by Gerhard Martin (Philadelphia: Fortress Press, 1976), p. xi.

29. John Edgerton, quoted in Harvey Swados, "Less Work—Less Leisure," in *Mass Leisure,* p. 354.

30. Wayne Oates, *Confessions of a Workaholic* (New York: World, 1971).

31. Although R. H. Tawney in his book *Religion and the Rise of Capitalism* (Magnolia, Mass.: Peter Smith, 1978) is somewhat critical of the methodology and implications of Max Weber's *The Protestant Ethic and the Spirit of Capitalism* (New York: Charles Scribner's Sons,

1978), Tawney does agree with Weber that the Calvinist-Puritan ethic gave impetus and sanction (sanctification?) to economic endeavors (p. 12).

32. Pierre Berton, *The Smug Minority* (Toronto: McClelland and Stewart, 1968), reported in William A. Sadler, Jr., "Creative Existence: Play as a Pathway to Personal Freedom and Community," *Humanitas,* 5 (Spring 1969), 58.

33. Richard M. Nixon, Labor Day Message, September 6, 1971, quoted in Gordon Dahl, *Work, Play, and Worship* (Minneapolis: Augsburg, 1972), p. 50.

34. Arnold W. Green, *Recreation, Leisure, and Politics* (New York: McGraw-Hill, 1964), p. 171.

35. U.S. Cong., *Work in America,* p. 4.

36. Walter Kerr, *The Decline of Pleasure* (New York: Simon & Schuster, 1962), pp. 39-40, 48.

37. Eric Hoffer, quoted in Brightbill, *Education for Leisure-Centered Living,* p. 164.

38. David M. Potter, *People of Plenty* (Chicago: University of Chicago Press, Phoenix Books, 1954), p. 60.

39. Yankelovich, *New Rules,* p. xvi.

40. *Ibid.,* p. 81.

41. Christopher Lasch, *The Culture of Narcissism: American Life in an Age of Diminishing Expectations* (New York: Norton, 1979).

42. Yankelovich, *New Rules,* p. 63.

43. *Ibid.,* p. 81.

44. Kerr, *The Decline of Pleasure,* p. 136.

45. Quoted by Richard Soles, "I'm Still Not Used to It," *Durham* (N.C.) *Morning Herald,* November 5, 1972, p. 4C.

46. Gabriel Vahanian, *Wait Without Idols* (New York: George Braziller, 1964), p. 42.

47. e.e. cummings, quoted in Theodore Roszak, *Where the Wasteland Ends: Politics and Transcendence in Post-Industrial Society* (Garden City, N.Y.: Doubleday, 1973), p. xiii.

48. Roszak, *Where the Wasteland Ends,* p. xix.

49. *Ibid.*

50. Buckminster Fuller, *Operating Manual for Spaceship Earth* (Boston: Massachusetts Institute of Technology Press, 1969), p. 91, quoted in Roszak, *Where the Wasteland Ends,* p. 13.

51. Raszak, *Where the Wasteland Ends,* pp. 70, 71, 91, 125.

52. *Ibid.,* pp. 232, 159, 381, 175, 233.

53. Kathleen Raine, quoted in Roszak, *Where the Wasteland Ends,* p. 242.

54. Gabriel Marcel, *Men Against Humanity* (London: Harvill Press, 1952), p. 1; also published as *Man Against Mass Society* (Chicago: Henry Tegnery, 1962), quoted in Sam Keen, *Gabriel Marcel,* Makers of Contemporary Theology Series, ed. D. E. Nineham and E. H. Robertson (Richmond, Va.: John Knox Press, 1967), p. 13.

55. Cf. Keen, *Gabriel Marcel,* p. 14.

56. James M. Houston, "The Loss and Recovery of the Personal," in *Quest for Reality: Christianity and the Counter Culture,* ed. Carl F. H. Henry (Downers Grove, Ill.: InterVarsity Press, 1973), p. 27.

57. *Ibid.,* pp. 23-24. Ellul is incisive in his criticism of contemporary society. However, as Harvey Cox points out, his writings are

incomplete because he fails to suggest a way out of man's social dilemma. Ellul wants us to disassociate ourselves from both "technique" and the "City" rather than seek to transform them. Ellul sees the present situation as hopeless. In this regard, he is at odds with those who see play (however broadly defined) as a possible means of cultural renewal and regeneration. Cf. Harvey Cox, *The Seduction of the Spirit: The Use and Misuse of People's Religion* (New York: Simon & Schuster, 1973), pp. 69-78.

58. Kerr, *The Decline of Pleasure,* pp. 23-24.

59. Walter J. Ong, Pref., *Man at Play,* by Hugo Rahner (New York: Herder & Herder, 1967), p. xiii.

60. Frederick Herzog, *Liberation Theology: Liberation in the Light of the Fourth Gospel* (New York: Seabury Press, 1972), p. 137.

61. In an article in 1970 which appeared in *Psychology Today,* Cox was asked how he reconciled what he said in *The Secular City* (1965) with what he later wrote in *The Feast of Fools* (1969). Cox responded: "So *Feast* is not a recantation of *Secular City*; it's an extension, a recognition that the changes we need are much more fundamental than I thought five years ago, and that the method for achieving them must be more drastic. Man actually took charge of his own history back in the 19th Century. In *City* I was trying to help us face that fact—defatalization—on the conscious level and work out the consequences. In *Feast* the point is that we can't handle the burden of making history if we are ourselves buried in it, unaware of the timeless dimension that we touch only in fantasy and festivity." From "Religion in the Age of Aquarius: A Conversation with Harvey Cox and T. George Harris," *Psychology Today,* April 1970, p. 62.

62. Cox, *The Seduction of the Spirit,* pp. 300, 282, 17, 11.

63. Rubem Alves, *Tomorrow's Child: Imagination, Creativity, and the Rebirth of Culture* (New York: Harper & Row, 1972), p. 1.

64. Wesley A. Kort, *Shriven Selves: Religious Problems in Recent American Fiction* (Philadelphia: Fortress Press, 1972), p. 10.

65. Cox, "Religion in the Age of Aquarius," p. 47.

66. C. S. Lewis, *The Abolition of Man* (New York: Macmillan, 1965).

67. Alves, *Tomorrow's Child,* p. 64.

68. *Ibid.,* p. 72.

CHAPTER TWO—PLAY:
A MATTER OF DEFINITION

1. George Sheehan, "Play," *American Way,* 10 (July 1977), 33.

2. *Random House Dictionary of the American Language* (New York: Random House, 1967), quoted in Richard Burke, " 'Work' and 'Play,' " *Ethics,* 82 (October 1971), 33.

3. Burke, " 'Work' and 'Play,' " p. 35. Cf. Eric Berne, *Games People Play* (New York: Grove Press, 1964); and Adam Smith (pseudonym), *The Money Game* (New York: Dell, 1969).

4. Sheehan, "Play," p. 33.

5. Walter J. Ong, Pref., *Man at Play,* by Hugo Rahner (New York: Herder & Herder, 1967), pp. ix-xi.

6. Johan Huizinga, *Homo Ludens: A Study of the Play Element in Culture* (Boston: Beacon Press, 1955), p. 7.

7. See Chapter One.

8. For a discussion of selected theories of play, see Robert E. Neale, *In Praise of Play* (New York: Harper & Row, 1969), pp. 19-41; David L. Miller, *Gods and Games: Toward a Theology of Play* (New York: World, 1970), pp. 17-94.

9. Rainer Maria Rilke, *Sonnets to Orpheus* (New York: Norton, 1942), I, 3.

10. Huizinga, *Homo Ludens*, p. 13.

11. Burke, " 'Work' and 'Play,' " pp. 37-38.

12. Jean Piaget, *Play, Dreams and Imitation in Childhood,* trans. C. Gattegno and F. M. Hodgson (New York: Norton, The Norton Library, 1962), pp. 92-93.

13. Neale, *In Praise of Play,* p. 97.

14. Rubem A. Alves, *Tomorrow's Child: Imagination, Creativity, and the Rebirth of Culture* (New York: Harper & Row, 1972), p. 98.

15. Jay B. Rohrlich, *Work and Love: The Crucial Balance* (New York: Summit Books, 1980), p. 72.

16. Plato, quoted in Josef Pieper, *In Tune with the World: A Theory of Festivity,* trans. Richard and Clara Winston (New York: Harcourt, Brace & World, 1965), p. 6.

17. Roger Bannister, *The Four Minute Mile* (New York: Dodd, Mead, 1957), p. 213.

18. Gerardus Van der Leeuw, *Sacred and Profane Beauty: The Holy in Art,* trans. David E. Green (New York: Abingdon Press, 1963), p. 280.

19. William A. Sadler, Jr., "Creative Existence: Play as a Pathway to Personal Freedom and Community," *Humanitas,* 5 (Spring 1969), 74.

20. Piaget, *Play, Dreams and Imitation,* p. 168; cf. Alves, *Tomorrow's Child,* p. 89.

21. Roy Harvey Pearce, "Historicism Once More," *The Kenyon Review,* 20 (Autumn 1958), 566; quoted in Giles B. Gunn, "Introduction: Literature and its Relation to Religion," in *Literature and Religion,* ed. Giles B. Gunn, Harper Forum Books, ed. Martin E. Marty (New York: Harper & Row, 1971), p. 24.

22. Huizinga, *Homo Ludens,* p. 213; cf. Walter Kerr, who, in his typically colorful style, makes this same point in *The Decline of Pleasure* (New York: Simon & Schuster, 1962), p. 239: "Our starving man apart, how much 'simple contemplation of its outward qualities' is likely to be given to a landscape or perhaps to the face of a pretty girl by a man who, though far from starving, has admitted into his mind the merest possibility of subdividing the landscape or seducing the girl? Even a very mild toying with the prospects of goodness—both the subdivision and the seduction have obvious goodness (or lack of it) about them—compromises the moment, rules out the pleasure that had nothing to do with profit." Cf. Michael Novak, *The Joy of Sports* (New York: Basic Books, 1976), pp. 278-280.

23. Thomas Langford, "Reclaiming the Human Spirit," lecture presented at the Divinity School of Duke University, Durham, N.C., February 17, 1972.

24. For a novel that forcefully portrays a player who becomes so consumed by a game that he must cheat in order to maintain his sanity,

see Robert Coover, *The Universal Baseball Association, Inc.: J. Henry Waugh, Prop.* (New York: New American Library, Signet Books, 1968).

25. William A. Sadler, Jr., "Play: A Basic Human Structure Involving Love and Freedom," *Review of Existential Psychology and Psychiatry,* 6 (Fall 1966), 243.

26. J. C. Friedrich von Schiller, *On the Aesthetic Education of Man,* trans. Reginald Snell (London: n.p., 1954), p. 137, quoted in Herbert Read, *The Redemption of the Robot: My Encounter with Education through Art* (New York: Trident Press, 1966).

27. Gabriel Vahanian, "Utopia as Ethic of Leisure," *Humanitas,* 8 (November 1972), 349.

28. Michelangelo Buonarroti, *Sonnets and Madrigals of Michelangelo Buonarroti,* quoted in Van der Leeuw, *Sacred and Profane Beauty,* p. 265.

29. Walter J. Ong, "Voice as Summons for Belief: Literature, Faith, and the Divided Self," in *Literature and Religion,* pp. 68-86.

30. Kerr, *The Decline of Pleasure,* p. 188.

31. Alves, *Tomorrow's Child,* p. 93.

32. Harvey Cox, *The Feast of Fools* (New York: Harper & Row, Colophon Books, 1969), p. 108.

33. This fact has often been obscured by those writing about play. Karl Rahner, for example, states: "The leisure of the Muse is free fall, the unplanned and unpredictable, confident surrender to the uncontrollable forces of existence, waiting for the irruption of the incalculable gift, the reception of grace, the aimless but meaningless hour" (*Theological Investigations,* trans. Kevin Smith [Baltimore: Helicon Press, 1966], IV, 379). On the other hand, critics of play such as Northrop Frye have recognized that "the quality that Italian critics called *Sprezzatura* and that Hoby's translation of Castiglione calls 'recklessness,' the sense of buoyancy or release [is] that [which] accompanies perfect discipline, when we can no longer know the dancer from the dance" (*Anatomy of Criticism* [Princeton: Princeton University Press, 1957], pp. 93-94).

34. Novak, *The Joy of Sports,* p. 224.

35. *Ibid.,* p. 225.

36. Huizinga, *Homo Ludens,* p. 188. Igor Stravinsky, in his *Poetics of Music in the Form of Six Lessons* (New York: Random House, Vintage Books, 1959), pp. 66-68, writes of the terror he feels at the thought that perhaps everything is permissible. In this situation the seven notes of the scale and its chromatic intervals provide him refuge against the threat of anomie. He says, "What delivers me from the anguish into which an unrestricted freedom plunges me is the fact that I am always able to turn immediately to the concrete things that are here in question. . . . My freedom will be so much the greater and more meaningful the more narrowly I limit my field of action."

37. Sheehan, "Play," p. 33.

38. Cox, *The Feast of Fools,* pp. 46-47.

39. Burke, " 'Work' and 'Play,' " p. 39.

40. Lee W. Gibbs, "Ritual, Play and Transcendent Mystery," paper presented to the American Academy of Religion, Midwestern Sectional Meeting, Chicago, Ill., February 17, 1973, p. 4.

41. Fred van Dyke, quoted in G. Rogin, "An Odd Sport . . . and an Unusual Champion," *Sports Illustrated,* October 18, 1965, p. 104.

42. Mark Lepper and David Greene, "Turning Play into Work," *Journal of Personality and Social Psychology,* 31 (1975), 479-486.

43. Novak, *The Joy of Sports,* p. 32.

44. Bill Bradley, *Life on the Run* (New York: Bantam Books, 1976), p. 236.

45. Robert Lee, *Religion and Leisure in America* (New York: Abingdon Press, 1964), p. 35.

46. Jurgen Moltmann, *Theology of Play,* trans. Reinhard Ulrich (New York: Harper & Row, 1972), p. 112.

47. Sheehan, "Play," p. 33.

48. Huizinga, *Homo Ludens,* p. 5; cf. Josef Pieper, *Leisure: The Basis of Culture,* trans. Alexander Dru (New York: Random House, 1964).

49. Vahanian, "Utopia as Ethic of Leisure," p. 352.

50. Charles M. Schulz, "Peanuts," quoted in Robert L. Short, *The Gospel According to Peanuts* (Richmond, Va.: John Knox Press, 1964), p. 112.

51. Kerr, *The Decline of Pleasure,* p. 223.

52. Bannister, *The Four Minute Mile,* pp. 11-12; cf. pp. 213-214.

53. Cox, *The Feast of Fools,* pp. 27-47.

54. Van der Leeuw, *Sacred and Profane Beauty,* pp. 104, 74, 259; cf. Joseph D. McLelland, *The Clown and the Crocodile* (Richmond, Va.: John Knox Press, 1970), pp. 71-76.

55. Judith Savard, *Full Circle, Our Second Edition* (New York: Full Circle Association, n.d.), n. pag.

56. Huizinga, *Homo Ludens,* p. 17.

57. Karl Barth, "Wolfgang Amadeus Mozart," in *Religion and Culture: Essays in Honor of Paul Tillich,* ed. Walter Leibrecht (New York: Harper & Brothers, 1959), p. 62. Cf. Donald E. Demaray, "Wolfgang Amadeus Mozart: A Man Through Whom God Sings," *The Asbury Seminarian,* 37 (Spring 1982), 15-19.

58. Rahner, *Theological Investigations,* IV, 384.

59. Novak, *The Joy of Sports,* p. 151.

60. John Updike, *Rabbit, Run* (Greenwich, Ct.: Fawcett Books, 1960), pp. 112-113; cf. John Updike, "Is There Life after Golf?", *New Yorker,* July 29, 1972, pp. 76-78.

61. Van der Leeuw, *Sacred and Profane Beauty,* p. 112.

62. Cox, *The Feast of Fools,* p. 186.

63. Rubem Alves, "More on Play," *Christianity and Crisis,* March 6, 1972, p. 45.

64. Alves, *Tomorrow's Child.*

65. John Cage, quoted in Mary Keelan, *Full Circle Playbook* (n.p.: Full Circle Association, 1970), p. 40.

66. Eric Gill, quoted in Kerr, *The Decline of Pleasure,* p. 277.

67. Ong, Pref., *Man at Play,* pp. ix-xi.

68. Charles K. Brightbill, *The Challenge of Leisure* (Englewood Cliffs, N.J.: Prentice-Hall, 1960), p. 7, quoted in Vahanian, "Utopia as Ethic of Leisure," p. 350.

69. Kerr, *The Decline of Pleasure,* p. 220.

70. Ernst Cassirer, *Essays on Man* (New York: n.p., 1953), n.p., quoted in Lawrence Meredith, *The Sensuous Christian* (New York: Association Press, 1972), p. 160. Cf. Cox, *The Feast of Fools,* p. 7.

71. Neale, *In Praise of Play,* pp. 70-82.

72. Kerr, *The Decline of Pleasure,* p. 278.

73. Huizinga, *Homo Ludens,* p. 206.

74. Cf. "The Olympic Landscape," *AIA Journal,* 58 (August 1972), 20-21.

75. Red Smith, "Show Goes On," *The Chronicle* (Duke University), *New York Times* News Service, September 7, 1972, p. 11; Heywood Hale Broun, "The 1984 Olympics," *Newsweek,* March 5, 1973, p. 13.

76. Dietrich Bonhoeffer, *Letters and Papers from Prison,* rev. ed., ed. Eberhard Bethge (New York: Macmillan, 1967), p. 155.

CHAPTER THREE — PLAY:
THREE THEOLOGICAL OPTIONS

1. W. H. Auden, *The Dyer's Hand and Other Essays* (New York: Random House, 1948), p. 409.

2. Sam Keen, *Apology for Wonder* (New York: Harper & Row, 1969); Sam Keen, "Manifesto for a Dionysian Theology," in *Transcendence,* ed. Herbert W. Richardson and Donald R. Cutler (Boston: Beacon Press, 1969), pp. 31-52; Sam Keen, *To a Dancing God* (New York: Harper & Row, 1970); Sam Keen and Anne Valley Fox, *Telling Your Story: A Guide to Who You Are and Who You Can Be* (Garden City, N.Y.: Doubleday, 1973).

3. Jurgen Moltmann, " 'How Can I Play, When I'm in a Strange Land?' ", *The Critic,* 29 (May-June 1971), 14-23; Jurgen Moltmann, "The First Liberated Men in Creation," in *Theology of Play,* responses by Robert E. Neale, Sam Keen, and David L. Miller (New York: Harper & Row, 1972). In *Theology of Play,* there is an interesting response to Moltmann's essay by Sam Keen entitled "godsong," and this in turn is followed by Moltmann's rebuttal, "Are there no rules of the Game?" Thus we have in this volume a brief but provocative dialogue between the theological left and the theological right on the topic of play.

4. Sam Keen, " 'We Have No Desire to Strengthen the Ego or Make It Happy': A Conversation about Ego Destruction with Oscar Ichazo," *Psychology Today,* July 1973, p. 67.

5. Keen, *Apology for Wonder,* p. 130.

6. *Ibid.,* p. 146.

7. Sam Keen, "Toward an Erotic Theology," in *Theology and Body,* ed. John Y. Fenton (Philadelphia: Westminster Press, 1974), p. 21; cf. Sam Keen, "My New Carnality," *Psychology Today,* October 1970, p. 59.

8. Keen, "My New Carnality," p. 59.

9. Keen, *Apology for Wonder,* p. 164.

10. Keen, *To a Dancing God,* p. 71.

11. Keen and Fox, *Telling Your Story,* p. 3.

12. Keen, *To a Dancing God,* p. 131.

13. Sam Keen, "Sing the Body Electric," *Psychology Today,* October 1970, p. 56.

14. Keen discusses *Homo Tempestivus* as a model of the authentic person in *Apology for Wonder,* pp. 190-199.

15. *Ibid.,* pp. 191, 192, 194, 195.

16. *Ibid.,* p. 198.

17. *Ibid.,* p. 201 (italics added).

18. *Ibid.,* p. 203.

19. Keen, *To a Dancing God*, pp. 137, 22, 99, 37, 138, 5, 123, 145, 118-20.

20. This is Keen's basic prescription both in his first major article, "Hope in a Posthuman Era," *The Christian Century*, January 25, 1967, pp. 106-109, and in his book *Apology for Wonder* (1969).

21. Keen, "Hope in a Posthuman Era," pp. 107-108.

22. Keen, *Apology for Wonder*, pp. 145-149.

23. *Ibid.*, p. 43.

24. Keen, *To a Dancing God*, pp. 99-100.

25. *Ibid.*, p. 100.

26. *Ibid.*, pp. 23, 144.

27. Keen and Fox, *Telling Your Story*, p. 29.

28. Keen, *To a Dancing God*, p. 159. Keen develops this theme in much of his writing for *Psychology Today*, where in such articles as "My New Carnality," "Sing the Body Electric," and " 'We do not have bodies, we are our bodies,' " Keen enlarges upon the need for visceral psychology, suggesting that such therapeutic practices as rolfing, bioenergetics, sensory awareness training, oriental body disciplines, dance, and the Alexander technique might offer man a cure for his dis-ease. See these articles in *Psychology Today*, October 1970, pp. 59-61; October 1970, pp. 56-58, 88; and September 1973, pp. 65-73, 98.

29. Sam Keen, "Toward an Erotic Theology," p. 32; cf. Keen, *To a Dancing God*, pp. 159, 144.

30. Rudolf Otto, *The Idea of the Holy: An Inquiry into the Non-Rational Factor in the Idea of the Divine and its Relation to the Rational*, trans. John W. Harvey (New York: Oxford University Press, 1958).

31. Keen, *Apology for Wonder*, p. 40.

32. *Ibid.*, pp. 204, 210, 206, 211.

33. Keen, *To a Dancing God*, p. 136.

34. *Ibid.*, p. 145.

35. *Ibid.*, pp. 12, 22-23, 27, 104, 115-117, 126, 136, 142-143.

36. *Ibid.*, p. 156.

37. Keen, *Apology for Wonder*, p. 175.

38. Keen, *To a Dancing God*, p. 79.

39. Keen and Fox, *Telling Your Story*, p. 68.

40. Jurgen Moltmann, "Freedom in the Light of Hope," baccalaureate sermon delivered at the Divinity School of Duke University, Durham, N.C., May 12, 1973, n.p.

41. Jurgen Moltmann, *The Theology of Hope: On the Ground and the Implications of a Christian Eschatology*, trans. James W. Leitch (New York: Harper & Row, 1967), p. 17.

42. Jurgen Moltmann, "The Revelation of God and the Question of Truth," in *Hope and Planning*, trans. Margaret Clarkson (New York: Harper & Row, 1971), p. 15.

43. Jurgen Moltmann, "Hope and Planning," in *Hope and Planning*, pp. 178-199.

44. Moltmann, *The Theology of Hope*, p. 203; Moltmann, "The Revelation of God," p. 18; Jurgen Moltmann, "The Realism of Hope: The Feast of the Resurrection and the Transformation of the Present Reality," *Concordia Theological Monthly*, 40 (March 1969), 153.

45. Daniel L. Migliore, rev. of *The Theology of Hope*, by Jurgen Moltmann, *Theology Today*, 25 (October 1968), 388-389.

46. Moltmann's response to his critics does not seem to have been an intentional one in a primary way. Rather than viewing Moltmann's thought on play as developing chiefly out of a dialogue with American theology, it would be better to conclude that (1) his systematic interest in exploring the various ramifications of a theology of hope led him to investigate ecclesiology, which he found playful, and (2) his desire to counteract the seriousness of student revolutionaries, both in Germany and in America, led him into a consideration of play as an antidote. He does, however, dedicate his essay to Harvey Cox, whom he calls a partner in this discussion, and thus he seems to have been aware of the direction in which some wanted him to move. Cf. Moltmann, Pref., *Theology of Play,* p. vii.

47. Moltmann has returned briefly to consider certain aspects of play in two of his later writings. *The Passion for Life: A Messianic Lifestyle* (Philadelphia: Fortress Press, 1978), pp. 50-81, treats the topics of friendship and of worship as feast. *The Church in the Power of the Spirit* (New York: Harper & Row, 1977), pp. 114-120, 261-275, takes up these same topics.

48. Moltmann, " 'How Can I Play?' ", p. 14; cf. Moltmann, "The First Liberated Men," pp. 1-3.

49. Moltmann, "The First Liberated Men," p. 69.

50. Moltmann, " 'How Can I Play?' ", pp. 16-18; cf. Moltmann, "The First Liberated Men," pp. 15-33.

51. Moltmann, "The First Liberated Men," pp. 33-34.

52. *Ibid.,* pp. 43-45, 48, 58.

53. *Ibid.,* pp. 48-49, 71, 36.

54. Moltmann, " 'How Can I Play?' ", p. 16.

55. Moltmann, "The First Liberated Men," p. 56.

56. *Ibid.,* pp. 15-24.

57. *Ibid.,* p. 19.

58. *Ibid.,* pp. 23-24.

59. Jurgen Moltmann, "Introduction to Christian Theology," ed. M. Douglas Meeks, Lectures in Christian Theology given at the Divinity School of Duke University, Durham, N.C., 1968, p. 241. Cf. Moltmann, *The Church in the Power of the Spirit,* p. 269.

60. Moltmann, " 'How Can I Play?' ", pp. 14, 16; cf. Moltmann, "The First Liberated Men," pp. 13, 71.

61. Che Guevara, quoted in Jurgen Moltmann, "God in Revolution," in *Religion, Revolution, and the Future*, trans. M. Douglas Meeks (New York: Charles Scribner's Sons, 1969), p. 143.

62. Moltmann, "The First Liberated Men," p. 13.

63. Moltmann, "God in Revolution," p. 147.

64. Moltmann, "The First Liberated Men," p. 13.

65. T. S. Eliot, *The Dry Salvages,* V (27-33), in *Four Quartets* (New York: Harcourt, Brace & Co., 1943), p. 27.

66. Peter L. Berger, *A Rumor of Angels: Modern Society and the Rediscovery of the Supernatural* (Garden City, N.Y.: Doubleday, Anchor Books, 1970), p. 47. In *The Heretical Imperative: Contemporary Possibilities of Religious Affirmation* (Garden City: N.Y.: Doubleday, Anchor Books, 1980), Berger again takes up his argument concerning the possibility of religious belief in our modern age. As in *A Rumor of Angels,* Berger's interest continues to be in the ways modern man "can try to uncover and retrieve the experiences embodied in [his religious] tradition" (p. xi). Moreover, in his preface he states he has in no way

changed his mind about the need to follow an inductive approach to explore the "signals of transcendence" to be found in human experience (p. ix).

67. Berger, *A Rumor of Angels,* pp. 52-53.
68. *Ibid.,* pp. 57-60, 64.
69. *Ibid.,* pp. 76, 83.
70. *Ibid.,* p. 89.
71. Berger, *The Heretical Imperative,* p. 58.
72. For a perceptive critique of Berger's theological "objectivity," see Gregory Baum, "Peter L. Berger's Unfinished Symphony," *Commonweal,* May 9, 1980, pp. 263-270: "In this argument then, it is Peter Berger who is imprisoned in modernity. Judged by the dominant biblical understanding of divine transcendence, Otto's idea of the Holy (which Berger adopts) and Berger's sacred canopy are not transcendent at all! ... In the Christian religion, theologians have argued, the doctrine that in Jesus Christ God is present to men and that the Holy Spirit transforms the face of the earth means that men need not leave history to encounter the transcendent God" (p. 267).
73. C. S. Lewis, *Surprised by Joy: The Shape of My Early Life* (New York: Harcourt, Brace & World, Harvest Books, 1955), pp. 170, 72, 168.
74. *Ibid.,* pp. 238, 180-181.
75. Cf. C. S. Lewis. "Christianity and Culture," reprinted in C. S. Lewis, *Christian Reflections,* ed. Walter Hooper (Grand Rapids, Mich.: Eerdmans, 1967), p. 23. Cf. the comment of Ransom, Lewis's protagonist in his science-fiction novel, *Out of the Silent Planet* (New York: Macmillan, 1965), p. 32: " 'Space' [was] a blasphemous libel for this empyrean ocean of radiance in which they swam. ... He had thought it barren: he saw now that it was the womb of worlds, whose blazing and innumerable offspring looked down nightly even upon the earth with so many eyes—and here, with how many more! No: Space was the wrong name. Older thinkers had been wiser when they named it simply the heavens—the heavens which declared the glory."
76. *Ibid.,* p. 34. Cf. C. S. Lewis, *An Experiment in Criticism* (Cambridge: Cambridge University Press, 1961), p. 19. In *Letters to Malcolm: Chiefly on Prayer* (New York: Harcourt, Brace & World, 1964), p. 90, Lewis describes this process as running "back up the sunbeam to the sun."
77. C. S. Lewis, "On Stories," in *Essays Presented to Charles Williams,* ed. C. S. Lewis (Grand Rapids, Mich.: Eerdmans, 1966), pp. 103, 101.
78. C. S. Lewis, "On Three Ways of Writing for Children," reprinted in C. S. Lewis, *Of Other Worlds,* ed. Walter Hooper (London: Geoffrey Bles, 1966), p. 30.
79. C. S. Lewis, Introd., *George MacDonald: An Anthology,* by George MacDonald, ed. C. S. Lewis (New York: Macmillan, 1954), pp. 16-17.
80. Lewis, *Surprised by Joy,* p. 179.
81. *Ibid.,* pp. 220, 180; Lewis, Introd., *George MacDonald,* pp. 16-17. Cf. Lewis's remarks in "The Weight of Glory": "The books or the music in which we thought the beauty was located will betray us if we trust in them; it was not *in* them, it only came *through* them and what came through them was longing, these things—the beauty, the memory of our own past—are good images of what we really desire;

but if they are mistaken for the thing itself, they turn into dumb idols. . . . For they are not the thing itself; they are only the scent of a flower we have not found, the echo of a tune we have not heard, news from a country we have never yet visited." C. S. Lewis, *"The Weight of Glory" and Other Addresses* (New York: Macmillan, 1949), pp. 4-5.

82. Lewis, *Surprised by Joy*, pp. 180, 220.

83. Cf. C. S. Lewis's comment: "I do not think the resemblance between the Christian and the merely imaginative experience is accidental. I think that all things, in their way, reflect heavenly truth, the imagination not the least." Quoted in Peter Kreeft, *C. S. Lewis: A Critical Essay* (Grand Rapids, Mich.: Eerdmans, 1969), p. 30.

84. Lewis, *Surprised by Joy*, p. 179.

85. *Ibid.*, p. 238.

86. Lewis, *Out of the Silent Planet*, p. 167.

87. *Ibid.*, pp. 29-30.

88. C. S. Lewis, *The Pilgrim's Regress* (Grand Rapids, Mich.: Eerdmans, 1958), p. 171.

89. C. S. Lewis, *The Lion, the Witch and the Wardrobe* (New York: Macmillan, Collier Books, 1970), pp. 42-45.

90. *Ibid.*, pp. 185-186.

91. C. S. Lewis, *The Voyage of the Dawn Treader* (New York: Macmillan, Collier Books, 1970), p. 209.

92. Walter Hooper, "On C. S. Lewis and the Narnian Chronicles," quoted in Eliane Tixier, "Imagination Baptized, or, 'Holiness' in the Chronicles of Narnia," in *The Longing for a Form: Essays on the Fiction of C. S. Lewis*, ed. Peter Schakel (Grand Rapids, Mich.: Baker Book House, 1979), p. 143.

93. Dietrich Bonhoeffer, *Letters and Papers from Prison*, enl. ed., ed. Eberhard Bethge (New York: Macmillan, 1971), p. 198.

CHAPTER FOUR—PLAY:
A BIBLICAL MODEL

1. Josef Pieper, *Leisure: The Basis of Culture*, trans. Alexander Dru (New York: Random House, Pantheon Books, 1964), p. 53.

2. William A. Sadler, Jr., "Creative Existence: Play as a Pathway to Personal Freedom and Community," *Humanitas*, 5 (Spring 1969), 72.

3. Lawrence Meredith, *The Sensuous Christian* (New York: Association Press, 1972), p. 157.

4. Margaret Mead, "The Pattern of Leisure in Contemporary American Culture," in *Mass Leisure*, ed. Eric Larrabee and Rolf Meyersohn (Glencoe, Ill.: Free Press, 1958), pp. 10-12.

5. Rudolph F. Norden, *The Christian Encounters the New Leisure* (St. Louis, Mo.: Concordia, 1965), pp. 70-88.

6. Bennett M. Berger, "The Sociology of Leisure: Some Suggestions," in *Work and Leisure: A Contemporary Social Problem*, ed. Erwin O. Smigel (New Haven, Conn.: College and University Press, 1963), p. 27.

7. Gregory Baum, "Peter L. Berger's Unfinished Symphony," *Commonweal*, May 9, 1980, p. 266.

8. Elmer W. K. Mould, *Essentials of Bible History* (New York: Thomas Nelson & Sons, 1941), pp. 278-279.

9. *Ibid.*

10. Alan Richardson, *The Biblical Doctrine of Work,* Ecumenical Biblical Studies, No. 1 (London: SCM Press, 1952), p. 53.

11. Leland Ryken, "In the Beginning God Created," in *The Christian Imagination,* ed. Leland Ryken (Grand Rapids, Mich.: Baker Book House, 1981), p. 57.

12. Josephus, *Antiquities,* XII, 6.

13. Paul Jewett, *The Lord's Day: A Theological Guide to the Christian Day of Worship* (Grand Rapids, Mich.: Eerdmans, 1971), p. 22.

14. Hans Walter Wolff, "The Day of Rest in the Old Testament," *Lexington Theological Quarterly,* 7 (July 1972), 66.

15. A. Alt, quoted in "The Day of Rest," p. 67.

16. Gerhard Von Rad, *Deuteronomy: A Commentary,* trans. Dorothea Barton, The Old Testament Library, ed. G. Ernest Wright and others (Philadelphia: Westminster Press, 1966), p. 58.

17. W. Gunther Plaut, "The Sabbath as Protest: Thoughts on Work and Leisure in the Automated Society," The B. G. Rudolph Lectures in Judaic Studies, Syracuse University, New York, April 1970, p. 10.

18. Jewett, *The Lord's Day,* p. 158. Cf. E. Jenni, *Die theologische Begrundung des Sabbatgebotes im Alten Testament* (Zollikon-Zurich: Evangelischer Verlag, 1956).

19. Alfred de Quervain, *Ethik,* Vol. 1: *Die Heiligung* (Zollikon-Zurich: Evangelischer Verlag, 1942), quoted in Jewett, *The Lord's Day,* p. 93.

20. Karl Barth, *Church Dogmatics,* Vol. III, 4: *The Doctrine of Creation,* ed. G. W. Bromiley and T. F. Torrance (Edinburgh: T. & T. Clark, 1961), 54.

21. Wayne Boulton, "Worship and Ethics: A Meditation on Isaiah 58," *The Reformed Journal,* September 1976, p. 11.

22. de Quervain, *Die Heiligung,* pp. 353-380.

23. de Quervain, quoted in Jewett, *The Lord's Day,* p. 93.

24. Barth, *Church Dogmatics,* III, 4, 57, 55. For Barth's complete discussion of the Sabbath, see pp. 47-72.

25. Cf. Jurgen Moltmann, *The Church in the Power of the Spirit* (New York: Harper & Row, 1977), pp. 269-270: "The weekly Sabbath is not merely ritual and symbol but an anticipation of the *shalom,* even if it is on the 'exceptional day.' The Sabbath is certainly part of the weekly cycle, but in its content it interrupts the cyclical rebirth of time by anticipating the Messianic era." Cf. Jurgen Moltmann, *The Passion for Life: A Messianic Lifestyle* (Philadelphia: Fortress Press, 1978), p. 76.

26. de Quervain, *Die Heiligung,* quoted in Barth, *Church Dogmatics,* III, 4, 51.

27. Barth, *Church Dogmatics,* III, 4, 56.

28. Jewett, *The Lord's Day,* p. 119.

29. At the Society of Biblical Literature, Southern Sectional Meeting, March 1974, I presented a paper on Qoheleth's underlying posture of joy. During the discussion which followed, James Crenshaw questioned how such an interpretation was possible, given Qoheleth's basic "pessimism" toward life, while John Priest argued instead that Qoheleth might best be understood as a "cynic."

30. Gerhard Von Rad, *Wisdom in Israel,* trans. James D. Martin (New York: Abingdon Press, 1972), pp. 227-228.

31. Robert Gordis, *Koheleth—The Man and His World,* 3rd aug. ed. (New York: Shocken Books, 1968), p. 131.

32. *Ibid.,* p. 119, quoted in Edwin Good, *Irony in the Old Testament* (Philadelphia: Westminster Press, 1965), p. 192.

33. Norbert Lohfink, *The Christian Meaning of the Old Testament,* trans. R. A. Wilson (Milwaukee: Bruce, 1968), pp. 154-155.

34. Lohfink, *The Christian Meaning of the Old Testament,* p. 152.

35. Von Rad, *Wisdom In Israel,* p. 265.

36. Although the meaning of the text is disputed, Ecclesiastes 12:11 provides collateral support for the pastoral emphasis of Ecclesiastes. As part of the concluding remarks of the book, verse 11 reads: "The sayings of the wise are like goads, and like nails firmly fixed are the collected sayings which are given by one Shepherd." It is unclear whether "shepherd" refers to God (as suggested by the RSV capitalization), or whether it refers to the sages (as other critics believe—e.g., Loretz). In either case, however, it is reasonable to conclude that Ecclesiastes as a wisdom book is being given a "pastoral" context by this statement.

37. Duncan Black Macdonald, *The Hebrew Philosophical Genius: A Vindication* (Princeton: Princeton University Press, 1936), p. 211. Unfortunately, Macdonald's insight is largely vitiated in his book by his misunderstanding of Qoheleth's view of God.

38. George S. Hendry, "Ecclesiastes," in *The New Bible Commentary,* rev. ed., ed. D. Guthrie and J. A. Motyer (Grand Rapids, Mich.: Eerdmans, 1970), pp. 570-571.

39. Although the text is disputed by biblical scholars, this interpretation of Qoheleth's thought lends strong support to the traditional rendering of Ecclesiastes 12:1, "Remember also your Creator in the days of your youth . . ." (RSV). Here, at the beginning of Qoheleth's summary poem (Eccl. 12:1-7), we find stated his underlying intent. Having tried to dispel man's false dreams, he calls man back to his rightful stance, that of being mindful of his Creator.

40. Qoheleth knows that there is much that mitigates against one's playful (joyful) work and play. There is, for this reason, a paradoxically "resigned" character to his emphasis on *simhah* (joy), for Qoheleth wishes that God would more fully reveal himself and his ways to him. Work and play are positive gifts from God, though Qoheleth always tempers this awareness with his recognition of humankind's ambiguous existence and God's inscrutable ways. In Qoheleth the "gift" of one's work or play is focused solely in the present. The larger dimensions of this "grace" remain for Qoheleth shrouded in mystery.

41. Harvey Cox, *The Seduction of the Spirit: The Use and Misuse of People's Religion* (New York: Simon & Schuster, 1973), p. 51.

42. Karl Barth, "Wolfgang Amadeus Mozart," in *Religion and Culture: Essays in Honor of Paul Tillich,* ed. Walter Leibrecht (New York: Harper & Brothers, 1959), pp. 67-73.

43. Karl Barth, *Church Dogmatics,* Vol. III, 2: *The Doctrine of Creation,* ed. G. W. Bromiley and T. F. Torrance (Edinburgh: T. & T. Clark, 1960), 294.

44. Otto A. Piper, *The Biblical View of Sex and Marriage* (New York: Charles Scribner's Sons, 1960), p. 30.

45. Jean Paul Audet, "Love and Marriage in the Old Testament," *Scripture,* 10 (July 1958), 76.

46. *Ibid.*, p. 78.

47. Karl Barth, *Church Dogmatics*, III, 2, 296-298.

48. Saint Jerome, quoted in Hugh J. Schonfield, *The Song of Songs* (New York: New American Library, Mentor Books, 1959), p. 12.

49. Mishnah, *Yadaim* 3:5.

50. Rabbi Akiba, quoted in Schonfield, *The Song of Songs*, p. 16.

51. Calvin Seerveld, *The Greatest Song: In Critique of Solomon* (Palos Heights, Ill.: Trinity Pennyasheet Press, 1967), p. 12.

52. Cyril of Alexandria, *Migne Graece* 69:1281.

53. Seerveld, *The Greatest Song*, p. 12.

54. *Ibid.*, p. 14.

55. H. H. Rowley, "The Interpretation of the Song of Songs," in *The Servant of the Lord and Other Essays on the Old Testament,* ed. H. H. Rowley (London: Lutterworth Press, 1952), p. 233.

56. E. J. Young, *An Introduction to the Old Testament* (Grand Rapids, Mich.: Eerdmans, 1949), p. 327.

57. W. J. Fuerst, *Ruth, Esther, Ecclesiastes, The Song of Songs, Lamentations,* The Cambridge Bible Commentary (New York: Cambridge University Press, 1975), p. 199.

58. Roland Murphy, "Towards a Commentary on the Song of Songs," *Catholic Biblical Quarterly,* 39 (1977), 487.

59. Jean Paul Audet, "Le sens du Cantique des Cantiques," *Revue biblique,* 62 (1955), 197-221.

60. M. H. Segal, "The Song of Songs," *Vetus Testamentum,* 12 (1962), 480.

61. Segal, "The Song of Songs," p. 483.

62. Hyam Maccoby, "Sex According to the Song of Songs," *Commentary,* 67 (June 1979), 54.

63. Jean Paul Audet, "Love and Marriage," p. 82.

64. For an excellent description of the great variety of love songs found in the Song, see Roland E. Murphy, *Wisdom Literature: Job, Proverbs, Ruth, Canticles, Ecclesiastes, Esther,* The Forms of the Old Testament Literature, Vol. XIII, ed. Rolf Knierim and Gene Tucker (Grand Rapids, Mich.: Eerdmans, 1981), pp. 105-124.

65. David A. Fraser, "Sensuous Theology," *The Reformed Journal,* February 1977, p. 22.

66. See Chapter Two.

67. Donald Bloesch, *The Struggle of Prayer* (San Francisco: Harper & Row, 1980), p. 157. Cf. Roland Murphy, "Towards a Commentary on the Song of Songs," pp. 495-496.

68. Murphy, "Towards a Commentary on the Song of Songs," pp. 495-496.

69. Bloesch, *The Struggle of Prayer,* p. 157.

70. J. Webb Mealy, "Some Thoughts on Old Testament Authropology as Reflected by the Concepts of Sabbath, Festival, and Dance," unpublished paper, July 1980.

71. The Hebrew word (*ḥāḡ*) for a pilgrimage festival seems to come from a circumambulating dance. Cf. the Muslim's annual pilgrimage to Mecca, the *ḥaj.*

72. The poet Heine comments, "Dancing was worship, a praying with the bones." Quoted by John Eaton, "Dancing in the Old Testament," *The Expository Times,* 86 (February 1975), 139.

73. Claus Westermann, "Work, Civilization and Culture in the Bible," in *Work and Religion,* Concilium Series, Vol. 131, ed. Gregory

Baum (New York: Seabury Press, 1980), pp. 85-86.

74. For a fuller discussion, see Robert K. Johnston, *Psalms for God's People* (Ventura, Ca.: Regal Books, 1982), chapter 6.

75. G. K. Chesterton, *Orthodoxy* (London: Collins, Fontana Books, 1961), p. 159.

76. Gary Warner, *Competition* (Elgin, Ill.: David C. Cook, 1979), p. 196.

77. I. H. Marshall, *The Gospel of Luke: A Commentary on the Greek Text*, The New International Greek Testament Commentary (Grand Rapids, Mich.: Eerdmans, 1978), p. 302.

78. Cf. Leon Morris, *The Gospel According to John*, The New International Commentary on the New Testament (Grand Rapids, Mich.: Eerdmans, 1971), p. 574: "It is difficult to escape the conclusion that Matthew, Mark, and John all refer to the same incident."

79. Immanuel Kant, "The Metaphysical Principles of Virtue," in *The Metaphysics of Morals* (Indianapolis: Bobbs-Merrill, 1964), p. 135. See Jurgen Moltmann, *The Passion for Life*, pp. 50-63, for a discussion of Christian friendship using Kant's ideas.

80. I. H. Marshall, *The Gospel of Luke*, p. 451.

81. Dietrich Bonhoeffer, *Letters and Papers from Prison*, enl. ed., ed. Eberhard Bethge (New York: Macmillan, 1971), p. 193.

CHAPTER FIVE—WORK:
ITS RELATIONSHIP TO PLAY

1. Cf. Jacques Ellul, *The Technological Society* (London: Cape, 1965), pp. 400-402; J. Dumazedier and N. Latouche, "Work and Leisure in French Sociology," *Industrial Relations*, 1 (February 1962), 13-30.

2. Kenneth Keniston, "Social Change and Youth in America," *Daedalus*, 91 (Winter 1962), quoted in Stanley Parker, *The Future of Work and Leisure* (New York: Praeger, 1971), p. 123.

3. Spiritual Statesmanship Conference, convened by the Jewish Theological Seminary of America. "Problems and Challenges of the New Leisure" (Boston: privately printed, 1956).

4. Bernard Mergen, "Work and Play in an Occupational Subculture: American Shipyard Workers, 1917-1977," in *Play: Anthropological Perspectives*, ed. Michael Salter (West Point, N.Y.: Leisure Press, 1978), p. 196.

5. Kunio Odaka, "Work and Leisure: As Viewed by Japanese Industrial Workers," quoted in Parker, *The Future of Work and Leisure*, p. 70.

6. Dorothy L. Sayers, *Creed or Chaos?* (New York: Harcourt, Brace, 1949), p. 53.

7. George Forell, "Work and the Christian Calling," *The Lutheran Quarterly*, 8 (May 1956), 109.

8. Forell, "Work and the Christian Calling," p. 116.

9. Cf. Karl Rahner, *Belief Today* (New York: Sheed & Ward, 1967), pp. 17-19.

10. Horace Bushnell, *Work and Play*, Literary Varieties, Vol. I (New York: Charles Scribner's Sons, 1881), p. 16.

11. Alan Richardson, *The Biblical Doctrine of Work*, Ecumenical Studies No. 1 (London: SCM Press, 1952), p. 19.

12. Sherwood Eliot Wirt, "Is Work So Holy?", *The Christian Century*, August 29, 1956, pp. 995-996. Cf. Jacques Ellul, *The Ethics of Freedom* (Grand Rapids, Mich.: Eerdmans, 1976), pp. 495-496: "Work is the painful lot of all men, but it is not particularly important. . . . I am not saying that work is bad. What I am saying is that its value is purely utilitarian and that it is one of the necessities of life."

13. Bengt R. Hoffman, "Theological Annotations on the Leisure-Work-Poverty Complex with an Ethical Postscript," *The Lutheran Quarterly*, 22 (August 1970), 244-245.

14. Gerard Manley Hopkins, *The Note-books and Papers,* ed. Humphrey House (New York: Oxford University Press, 1937), pp. 304-305.

15. Lewis Smedes, "Theology and the Playful Life," in *God and the Good,* ed. Clifton Orlebeke and Lewis Smedes (Grand Rapids, Mich.: Eerdmans, 1975), pp. 46-62.

16. Lewis Smedes, "Toward a Theology of Playfulness," unpublished draft of "Theology and the Playful Life."

17. Smedes, "Theology and the Playful Life," p. 60.

18. George E. Vaillant, *Adaptation to Life* (Boston: Little, Brown, 1977), p. 373.

19. Jay Rohrlich, *Work and Love: The Crucial Balance* (New York: Summit Books, 1980), p. 23.

20. Personal interview with Charles Garfield, Berkeley, California, April 1981.

CONCLUSION

1. F. Burton Nelson, Vice-President of the Bonhoeffer Society, is working on an oral history project about Bonhoeffer's acquaintances, and confirms the fact that Bonhoeffer's humanity, even more than his theology, has had the greatest lasting influence on his friends.

2. Wolf-Dieter Zimmermann, "Years in Berlin," in *I Knew Dietrich Bonhoeffer,* ed. Wolf-Dieter Zimmermann and Ronald Gregor Smith (London: Collins, Fontana Books, 1973), pp. 59-67. Cf. Theodore A. Gill, "Bonhoeffer as Aesthete" (unpublished paper).

3. Albrecht Schönherr, "The Single-Heartedness of the Provoked," in *I Knew Dietrich Bonhoeffer,* pp. 126-129.

4. Dietrich Bonhoeffer, "After Ten Years," *Letters and Papers from Prison,* rev. ed., ed. Eberhard Bethge (New York: Macmillan, 1967), pp. 4, 13.

5. Bonhoeffer, prison letter of January 29 and 30, 1944, *Letters and Papers from Prison,* p. 108.

6. *Ibid.*

7. Bonhoeffer, prison letter of May 20, 1944, *Letters and Papers from Prison,* p. 150.

8. Bonhoeffer, prison letter of January 23, 1944, *Letters and Papers from Prison,* p. 104.

9. Bonhoeffer, "The Friend," *Letters and Papers from Prison,* pp. 209-210.

Selected Bibliography
On Play (and Work)

Alves, Rubem. *Tomorrow's Child: Imagination, Creativity, and the Rebirth of Culture.* New York: Harper & Row, 1972.

Bannister, Roger. *The Four Minute Mile.* New York: Dodd, Mead, 1957.

Barth, Karl. *Church Dogmatics,* Vol. III, 2, 3, 4: *The Doctrine of Creation.* Ed. G. W. Bromiley and T. F. Torrance. Edinburgh: T. & T. Clark, 1960-1961.

——————. "Wolfgang Amadeus Mozart." In *Religion and Culture: Essays in Honor of Paul Tillich.* Ed. Walter Leibrecht. New York: Harper & Brothers, 1959, pp. 67-73.

Baum, Gregory, ed. *Work and Religion.* Concilium Series, Vol. 131. New York: Seabury Press, 1980.

Berger, Peter L. *The Heretical Imperative: Contemporary Possibilities of Religious Affirmation.* Garden City, N.Y.: Doubleday, Anchor Books, 1980.

——————. *A Rumor of Angels: Modern Society and the Rediscovery of the Supernatural.* Garden City, N.Y.: Doubleday, Anchor Books, 1970.

Bonhoeffer, Dietrich. *Letters and Papers from Prison.* Rev. ed. Ed. Eberhard Bethge. New York: Macmillan, 1967.

Bradley, Bill. *Life on the Run.* New York: Bantam Books, 1976.

Brown, Robert McAfee. *The Pseudonyms of God.* Philadelphia: Westminster Press, 1972.

Burke, Richard. " 'Work' and 'Play.' " *Ethics,* 82 (October 1971), 33-47.

Bushnell, Horace. *Work and Play.* Literary Varieties, Vol. I. New York: Charles Scribner's Sons, 1881.

Coover, Robert. *The Universal Baseball Association, Inc.: J. Henry Waugh, Prop.* New York: New American Library, Signet Books, 1968.

Cox, Harvey. *The Feast of Fools.* New York: Colophon Books, 1969.

——————. *The Seduction of the Spirit: The Use and Misuse of People's Religion.* New York: Simon & Schuster, 1973.

Dahl, Gordon. *Work, Play, and Worship.* Minneapolis: Augsburg, 1972.

Hoch, Paul. *Rip Off: The Big Game.* New York: Doubleday, Anchor Books, 1973.

Huizinga, Johan. *Homo Ludens: A Study of the Play Element in Culture.* Boston: Beacon Press, 1955.

Jewett, Paul. *The Lord's Day: A Theological Guide to the Christian Day of Worship.* Grand Rapids, Mich.: Eerdmans, 1971.

Johnston, Robert K. " 'Confessions of a Workaholic': A Reappraisal of Qoheleth." *Catholic Biblical Quarterly,* 38 (January 1976), 14-28.

Kaplan, Max, and Philip Bosserman, eds. *Technology, Human Values and Leisure.* New York: Abingdon Press, 1971.

Keen, Sam. *Apology for Wonder.* New York: Harper & Row, 1969.

_____. "Manifesto for a Dionysian Theology," in *Transcendence.* Ed. Herbert W. Richardson and Donald R. Cutler. Boston: Beacon Press, 1969, pp. 31-52.

_____. *To a Dancing God.* New York: Harper & Row, 1970.

_____. "Toward an Erotic Theology," In *Theology and Body.* Ed. John Y. Fenton. Philadelphia: Westminster Press, 1974, pp. 13-37.

Keen, Sam, and Anne Valley Fox. *Telling Your Story: A Guide to Who You Are and Who You Can Be.* Garden City, N.Y.: Doubleday, 1973.

Kerr, Clark, and Jerome Rosaw, eds. *Work in America: The Decade Ahead.* Work in America Institute Scribes. New York: Van Nostrand, 1979.

Kerr, Walter. *The Decline of Pleasure.* New York: Simon & Schuster, 1962.

Larrabee, Eric, and Rolf Meyersohn, eds. *Mass Leisure.* Glencoe, Ill.: Free Press, 1958.

Lasch, Christopher. *The Culture of Narcissism: American Life in an Age of Diminishing Expectations.* New York: Norton, 1979.

Lee, Robert. *Religion and Leisure in America.* New York: Abingdon Press, 1964.

Lepper, Mark, and David Greene. "Turning Play into Work." *Journal of Personality and Social Psychology,* 31 (1975), 479-486.

Lewis, C. S. *The Abolition of Man.* New York: Macmillan, 1965.

_____, ed. *Essays Presented to Charles Williams.* Grand Rapids, Mich.: Eerdmans, 1966.

_____. *The Lion, the Witch and the Wardrobe.* New York: Macmillan, Collier Books, 1970.

_____. *Of Other Worlds.* Ed. Walter Hooper. London: Geoffrey Bles, 1966.

_____. *Out of the Silent Planet.* New York: Macmillan, 1965.

_____. *Surprised by Joy: The Shape of My Early Life.* New York: Harcourt, Brace & World, Harvest Books, 1955.

Linder, Staffan Burenstam. *The Harried Leisure Class.* New York: Columbia University Press, 1970.

Martin, Gerhard. *Fest: The Transformation of Everyday.* Philadelphia: Fortress Press, 1976.

McLelland, Joseph D. *The Clown and the Crocodile.* Richmond, Va.: John Knox Press, 1970.

Meredith, Lawrence. *The Sensuous Christian.* New York: Association Press, 1972.

Michener, James. *Sports in America.* New York: Random House, 1976.

Miller, David L. *Gods and Games: Toward a Theology of Play.* New York: World, 1970.

Moltmann, Jurgen. *The Church in the Power of the Spirit.* New York: Harper & Row, 1977.

──────────. *The Passion for Life: A Messianic Lifestyle.* Philadelphia: Fortress Press, 1978.

──────────. *Theology of Play.* Trans. Reinhard Ulrich. New York: Harper & Row, 1972.

Murphy, Roland E. *Wisdom Literature: Job, Proverbs, Ruth, Canticles, Ecclesiastes, Esther.* The Forms of the Old Testament Literature, Vol. XIII. Ed. Rolf Knierim and Gene Tucker. Grand Rapids, Mich.: Eerdmans, 1981.

Neale, Robert E. *In Praise of Play.* New York: Harper & Row, 1969.

Norden, Rudolph F. *The Christian Encounters the New Leisure.* St. Louis, Mo.: Concordia, 1965.

Novak, Michael. *The Joy of Sports.* New York: Basic Books, 1976.

Oates, Wayne. *Confessions of a Workaholic.* New York: World, 1971.

Orlebeke, Clifton, and Lewis Smedes, eds. *God and the Good.* Grand Rapids, Mich.: Eerdmans, 1975.

Parker, Stanley. *The Future of Work and Leisure.* New York: Praeger, 1971.

Pfeffer, Richard M. *Working for Capitali$m.* New York: Columbia University Press, 1979.

Piaget, Jean. *Play, Dreams and Imitation in Childhood.* Trans. C. Gattegno and F. M. Hodgson. New York: Norton, The Norton Library, 1962.

Pieper, Josef. *In Tune with the World: A Theory of Festivity.* Trans. Richard and Clara Winston. New York: Harcourt, Brace & World, 1965.

──────────. *Leisure: The Basis of Culture.* Trans. Alexander Dru. New York: Random House, Pantheon Books, 1964.

Plaut, W. Gunther. "The Sabbath as Protest: Thoughts on Work and Leisure in the Automated Society." The B. G. Rudolph Lectures in Judaic Studies. Syracuse University, New York. April 1970.

Rahner, Hugo. *Man at Play.* New York: Herder & Herder, 1967.

Richardson, Alan. *The Biblical Doctrine of Work.* Ecumenical Biblical Studies, No. 1. London: SCM Press, 1952.

Rohrlich, Jay B. *Work and Love: The Crucial Balance.* New York: Summit Books, 1980.

Roszak, Theodore. *Where the Wasteland Ends: Politics and Transcen-*

dence in Post-Industrial Society. Garden City, N.Y.: Doubleday, 1973.

Ryken, Leland, ed. *The Christian Imagination.* Grand Rapids, Mich.: Baker Book House, 1981.

Sadler, William A., Jr. "Creative Existence: Play as a Pathway to Personal Freedom and Community." *Humanitas,* 5 (Spring 1969), 57-79.

_____ . "Play: A Basic Human Structure Involving Love and Freedom." *Review of Existential Psychology and Psychiatry,* 6 (Fall 1966), 237-245.

Salter, Michael, ed. *Play: Anthropological Perspectives.* West Point, N.Y.: Leisure Press, 1978.

Sayers, Dorothy L. *Creed or Chaos?* New York: Harcourt, Brace, 1949.

Schall, James V. *Far Too Easily Pleased: A Theology of Play, Contemplation and Festivity.* Beverly Hills: Benziger, 1976.

Seerveld, Calvin. *The Greatest Song: In Critique of Solomon.* Palos Heights, Ill.: Trinity Pennyasheet Press, 1967.

Segal, M. H. "The Song of Songs." *Vetus Testamentum,* 12 (1962), 480.

Terkel, Studs. *Working.* New York: Random House, Pantheon Books, 1974.

U. S. Cong. Senate. Committee on Labor and Public Welfare, Subcommittee on Employment, Manpower, and Poverty. *Work in America,* report of a special task force to the Secretary of Health, Education, and Welfare. 93rd Cong., 1st sess. Washington, D.C.: GPO, 1973.

Vaillant, George E. *Adaptation to Life.* Boston: Little, Brown, 1977.

Van der Leeuw, Gerardus. *Sacred and Profane Beauty: The Holy in Art.* Trans. David E. Green. New York: Abingdon Press, 1963.

Warner, Gary. *Competition.* Elgin, Ill.: David C. Cook, 1979.

Wolff, Hans Walter. "The Day of Rest in the Old Testament." *Lexington Theological Quarterly,* 7 (July 1972), 65-76.

Yankelovich, Daniel. *New Rules: Searching for Self-Fulfillment in a World Turned Upside Down.* New York: Random House, 1981.

Zimmermann, Wolf-Dieter, and Ronald Gregor Smith, eds. *I Knew Dietrich Bonhoeffer.* London: Collins, Fontana Books, 1973.